JOURNEY *of* MIRACLES

Faith Adventures of a Tribal Woman from India

AMONGLA SETEFANO

INDIA · SINGAPORE · MALAYSIA

All Scripture quotations in this book are from the
New International Version (NIV).

This book is dedicated to my husband, Tai Setefano,
who stood faithfully with me through our years
together, and to all who follow Christ.

Contents

Acknowledgements

This book stands tall on the shoulders of those whose guidance and support fueled its creation. In the journey of bringing this publication to fruition, a heartfelt thank you is owed to my editor, Mr. Scott Tompkins from the USA, for his unwavering support, dedication of time, and invaluable suggestions. It is undeniable that without his guidance and persistent assistance, the realization of this book would have remained but a distant dream. Mr. Scott's genuine commitment to this project has been the cornerstone of its success. His honesty, thoughtful suggestions, and expert advice have not only shaped the direction of this book but have also sparked a transformation in my approach and perspective. Each interaction with Mr. Scott has been a catalyst for innovation, driving me to redefine and refine my ideas with renewed vigor and enthusiasm.

I would like to extend my heartfelt appreciation to my friend, professor Jen, for consistently offering her moral support and for her help with proofreading. My niece, professor Purlemla, also gave invaluable assistance in proofreading. Lis C. has been as invaluable source of encouragement and motivation throughout my journey. I am grateful for her steadfast encouragement. There are many people who enabled me to write this book. To every individual who has played a part in my journey or prayed for me, I extend my deepest thanks. Your contributions have been the cornerstone of my success, and I am profoundly grateful for your unwavering presence.

I am deeply grateful to my late parents, whose constant prayers served as a guiding light in every step of my journey. Their love, wisdom, and constant support continue to inspire me, even in their absence. Their presence may no longer be physical, but their spirit lives on, a source of strength and motivation in all that I do.

To my family members and relatives, I extend heartfelt appreciation for being the sturdy pillars beneath my wings. Your unwavering belief in me, your encouragement, and your consistent support have been the bedrock upon which I've built my dreams. In moments of doubt or uncertainty, your presence has provided comfort and reassurance, reminding me that I am never alone in my endeavors.

Above all, I thank God for each and everything.

Introduction

I grew up in the lush, green hills of rural Nagaland India. Born into a humble home, where love and laughter were abundant but where financial struggles often loomed like shadows in the background, I felt the weight of responsibility settling on my small shoulders as I watched my parents work tirelessly to provide for our family, but the income was never quite enough. Determined to help ease their burden, I set out to make something of myself, to secure a stable future not just for myself but for my parents and siblings, as well.

As I undertook this responsibility, however, I felt a stirring deep within my soul, a calling that whispered in the quiet moments of the night. It was a calling I couldn't quite understand, couldn't quite grasp, but I knew I couldn't ignore. The words of God's call to Abraham in Genesis 12:1 captured my attention: "The Lord had said to Abram, 'Leave your country, your people and your father's household and go to the land I will show you.'" Through this verse, God was speaking to me, guiding me, showing me the path I was meant to walk. From that day forward, I took on a new purpose. Though the dreams of financial success still lingered in the back, I found myself drawn to a different kind of success, a success measured not in wealth or status, but in the lives to touch and the hearts to be healed by sharing God's love.

This journey took me to places I had never imagined, to cities bustling with life and to remote villages tucked away in the mountains. Along the way, I met people from all walks of life, people who were broken and lost, people who were searching for something they couldn't quite name. In each of those encounters, I realized that this was my calling, the true purpose in life – to be a vessel for God's love, to spread His message of hope and redemption to every corner of the earth.

Though the journey was long and the road often rocky, I put my faith in God, for I knew that God had a plan, a plan far greater than anything I could have ever imagined. And as I looked back on the little girl I once was, I realized that every twist and turn, every triumph and trial, had led me to exactly where I was meant to be – in the loving arms of her Creator, fulfilling destiny as a messenger of His grace.

In sharing my story, I hope to inspire youth to embrace the unexpected twists and turns of life's journey, understanding that sometimes our dreams may lead us down paths we never imagined. And, in all this, God's purpose unfolds. "Trust in the Lord with all your heart and lean not on your own understanding; in all your ways acknowledge him, and he will make your paths straight" (Proverbs 3:5-6).

Chapter 1
When Jesus Stepped In

"Amongla, get up! We need to move quickly." I strained to see my mother Amenla's work-hardened face in the morning darkness. "Oh, (Oja) mother, let me sleep a little longer."

"No, Lanu is ready and needs your help. I need firewood for the stove," she said, pulling me up from my bamboo bed in one fluid motion. Tired as I was, I knew I had to obey. My father would never permit any laziness. By the time the dawn splashed sunlight on the green mountains above our village, my brother Lanu and I were up gathering firewood and toting water for our family's breakfast.

Our mountain village of Molungkimong consists of about 200 bamboo and palm-thatched homes, none of which have electricity or running water. Village children in our isolated part of South Asia face an early choice in life: work hard or starve.

Our parents are poor rice farmers, scratching out a living in fields carved from the jungle. Though Molungkimong is part of Nagaland, a far eastern state of India, it bears a closer resemblance to the neighbouring nations of Bhutan, Bangladesh, and Burma (Myanmar).

By the age of about 14, I was assigned several daily tasks, carrying water being the worst. I longed for the day when my three younger sisters (Yashila, Asenla, and Atenla) were strong enough to help. Daily at the early hour of sunrise, at 5 a.m., my brother Lanu and I trek to a spring to bring home water in five-foot-long bamboo carriers that we hitch to our heads and back.

Our humble house has just large one room where we all sleep on one side. The other side has a kitchen and bathroom, both made of our most common resource—bamboo. Mother sets to work boiling black tea the moment we arrive with firewood and water. "Come and sit," my father summons us. "Mother has rice for you, and a bit of vegetables." I watch as my brother—slender and brown from working hard in the rice field—gulps down his portion. Mother makes sure we all get an equal amount even though my brother Lanu works harder than all his sisters.

Soon we are off to school, which is taught in my mother's Ao tongue. After school, my parents expect us to rush home, drop our books, and hurry to the rice field to help them. I admire my parents, who work so hard to feed and care for us. They anticipate that the five of us will follow in the footsteps of their parents and grandparents, who were farmers who loved and worked the land

I have a bigger dream. I want to study to be a nurse or a teacher. But after an exhausting day of work carrying water, going to school, and tending the rice paddy, I have no energy for extra reading or homework. I often fall asleep soon after our dinner.

Once, our village was hit by a severe famine. Rice paddies dried up and all of us in the village struggled to obtain enough food. My father went into the jungle to search for food and sometimes he would bring home jungle potatoes. Often, he went fishing, and even the smallest fish he brought home was a great treat for us. Mother made it into a fine fish curry.

As the famine worsened, my father searched for work in a town called Tuli, where my aunty lives. It was a two-hour walk for him to get there, but he was able to get a job cutting wood. With the money he earned, he bought rice for us, which Mother cooked and then shared in equal portions.

Two of my friends come from a single-parent family living on our street, and they had no rice at all. So, I gave them half of my portion, wrapped in banana leaves that I discreetly passed to them from my balcony.

My parents taught me to share with needy people, but my concern for others grew mostly from things

I learned in Sunday school. Our village is famous in Nagaland as the first place where Christianity was established. An American Baptist missionary named Dr. Edward Clark set to work transcribing the Ao language into written script and started the area's first school in 1872.

One night there was a crusade at the church, and I decided to go. "Come with me, mother, I hear the speaker is very good."

"No, you go. Take your sisters if any of them want to go."

None did, and sadly, because that was the most significant night of my life. The preacher spoke about receiving salvation through Jesus Christ. At the end of the service, he gave an altar call. I don't know what happened to me, but my tired legs carried me in front. I felt convicted about my sins, and I repented of them. I accepted Jesus Christ as my personal savior, and I made a commitment to serve God. That was a moment I will never forget. I had such joy and serenity. It was the first love I had, feeling the delight of the Lord in my heart.

I came home from church smiling and singing. "What happened to you?" my mother asked.

"I gave my heart to Jesus, and I feel so happy," I said.

Mother didn't seem to know what to say. She just nodded and went back to her sewing.

From that point, I attended church every time I could. I loved talking to God, and a friend introduced me to two women who became my prayer partners. They were much older than me, and I felt encouraged by them right away. Every Friday we fasted and prayed. God answered our prayers because we had faith and believed in his Word.

Soon after, I had a dream that one day I would become a full time Christian worker. But how? When? I had no financial support and very little encouragement from my family. Yet, in my simple faith, I knew one day God would make a way for me.

I also prayed he would help with the more pressing issue of helping to support our family financially. As the eldest daughter, I felt this as a daily weight.

I don't remember my parents ever giving me money for my needs. Like my sisters, I had just two dresses, which my mother considered adequate. She taught me to weave cotton threads into our traditional Ao dress and wrap-around skirts. It took three weeks of working with the threads on the loom to make one skirt with our traditional patterns woven inside. I also learned to weave natural materials into bags. I sold these items for money.

Every day I prayed, "Lord, help me work hard and get earn money for my study and my needs, as well as to help my siblings." I didn't know it then, but God was going to teach me that his ways of finances were much different than mine.

Figure 1   The house I grew up in was very similar to this bamboo structure.

Chapter 2
A Brush with Death

That year, I had a desire to see Dimapur, the largest city in Nagaland. Some of my cousins were working in a sugar mill, and they invited me to come for a visit.

On the day I arrived in Dimapur, my cousins welcomed me to their small but nice family house, which was provided to them by the sugar mill company. It was summer, and the heat and humidity made me feel like I would melt at any moment. Even so, my cousin Amenla wanted to show me the city and took me to the downtown area. Dimapur is tiny compared to the great cities of India like Mumbai and New Delhi, but Amenla thought it was a grand place. After walking around a bit, we both were soaked in sweat.

"Let's go get something to drink," she suggested. So, she took me into a hotel and ordered two cold *lassis*, a yoghurt-based drink that's popular throughout India. I was a little concerned because the hotel was swarming with flies and didn't look particularly clean. But we both were so hot that we decided to have a lassi before heading back to the house.

Within a few minutes, my stomach started making a growling sound, followed by dizziness and pain like I'd never experienced before.

"I don't feel good. I need to go to the toilet," I moaned to Amenla.

She guided me to the nearest toilet, and I immediately started retching and vomiting. My head was spinning, and I felt like I'd been kicked in the stomach.

"Please Amenla, let's go home! I need to lay down."

She rushed out and secured an auto rickshaw (small vehicle). I continued to vomit on the way back to the house, which thankfully was just a short drive away. I didn't know it at the time, but I was suffering from the deadly disease, cholera. Amenla and others helped me into bed, and within a few minutes, I fell unconscious.

When I no longer responded to her, Amenla looked terrified.

"I think she may be dying," she said to cousin Odi Alem. "What should we do?"

"We need to get her to the hospital," he said.

Together my cousins lifted me into an auto rickshaw and rushed me to a local Catholic hospital. I was admitted, but doctors and nurses questioned whether I would live to the next day. Cholera, which is caused by unsanitary conditions, kills thousands each year. It causes uncontrolled vomiting and diarrhoea. Subsequent dehydration often sends the body into shock.

The doctor said to Odi Alem, "You need to contact her family. She is getting weaker by the hour, and we don't have much hope that she will survive. I suggest you take her home and prepare for a funeral."

"I will call her parents," he replied, "But I am not taking her back home. Give her the best care you can. If she dies, let her die in the hospital."

The doctor nodded and motioned for the nurses to pump more fluids into my body.

When he got the news, my father asked people at my church to pray for me, then he hurried to Dimapur by bus to the hospital. Thankfully, many did pray, crying out to God for my life. Throughout the next six days, my body was wracked by diarrhoea and fever. When I finally could open my eyes, I asked Odi Alem, "Where am I?"

"You have been in the hospital for last six days. You nearly died from cholera."

"Ohhhh," I groaned. "I feel so weak."

"Yes, but you are alive. God has answered our prayers."

I flashed a smile and touched his hand. Then I said to him, "Right before I opened my eyes, I saw a white cloud on the ceiling inside my hospital room. From it, I heard a voice say to me, 'Amongla, will you continue to serve me?' I knew it was the voice of God that I had heard. I said, 'Yes, I will, Lord.'"

News of my awakening spread like floodwaters in monsoon season. Within minutes, my room was full of nurses, doctors, and relatives, all eager to see me awake again and to hear how I was feeling. I thanked them for their care, and I told them about the significant voice I had heard. Several seemed surprised to see me speaking again. "It is a miracle that I am alive," I told them. Several cholera patients had died at that hospital.

They kept me in there for a few more days. I kept praying for quick recovery and by the grace of God, I gained a little more strength each day. After I was discharged from the hospital, I stayed for a week at Odi Alem's house. I was still feeling weak, but my father took me home.

My mother, brother, and sisters all happily gave praise to God. Within a few weeks, I recovered enough to get back to work, but I knew I would soon be keeping my promise to God, doing whatever work he was calling me to do.

Chapter 3
A Life-Changing School

I knew God had spared my life for a reason, and I was full of hunger and dreams of becoming a full-time full time Christian worker. That seemed so impossible for a girl from a poor family in rural Nagaland, but God soon taught me that all things are possible to those who exercise their gift of faith.

As a teenager, I got a job in the accounts office at a paper mill to support my siblings and my parents financially. I also helped part-time as a Sunday school teacher at the Tzudikong Baptist Church, Tuli. I loved teaching the children Bible stories, new songs, and choreography. I wondered if this was the kind of work God was calling me to, and I began to pray earnestly about my future. Although I was getting a salary from the paper mill and supporting my siblings, I had no peace, no satisfaction.

After expressing my frustration, a coworker asked, "Amongla, what kind of work do *you* want to do?"

"I want to tell others about Jesus. I want to serve him full-time in missions." I didn't know exactly what that meant, but I hoped God would show me.

One day my friend, Mr. Onen said, "I think you need to join Youth With A Mission and do a DTS."

"What's a DTS?" I asked.

"It's a Discipleship Training School to help people get to know the ways of God and to show them how to tell others about Jesus." I got so excited. Mr. Onen had just completed a DTS, and he told me how blessed he was by it.

"That sounds perfect for me. Where is this school?"

"I know they have one in Uluberia Kolkata."

The more I learned about it, the more I knew I wanted to enrol in this school. I sent my application, but I was concerned because some of the teaching would be in English, and my language skills were poor. After a few weeks, I was surprised to receive an acceptance letter from a Y centre in Bangalore.

As long as I got in, I didn't care where I'm enrolled. I was just thankful the Lord had opened the door for me. In July 1995, I took leave from my job and headed to Bangalore with my friend Mapula. She is much older than me. It was the first time I had travelled out of Nagaland, and the journey to southern India took four miserable days by train. The weather was sticky and hot, and the wretched smells on the crowded train made it hard to breathe.

The trains stop for only a few minutes in each station so, when we got to Bangalore, we literally had to jump off the train. When I jumped, I believed Mapula was behind me, but she wasn't. I observed someone go down the steps into a pile of bags as the train was leaving. Mapula was the one!

"Are you alright?" I asked

"Yes, my knee hurts, but I think I can walk." Said Mapula

"I'm so thankful. This is not the kind of start I hoped for."

We hired an auto rickshaw to take us to the Y Bangalore base in Kammanahalli. The week before we left, I had a dream about the colour and shape of the building. When we reached Kammanahalli, the Y centre looked exactly as I pictured it in my dream. The staff greeted us and showed us to our simple room which included bunk beds, a small table, and a welcome basket for each of us. The basket contained fruit, snacks, and a personal note with scripture quotations.

My biggest adjustment at first was the food! South Indian food—with its oily, coconut-based curries—is so different from the simple fare of my native Nagaland. I couldn't eat it at first but, after a few weeks, I began to like it.

Meanwhile, I thoroughly enjoyed the "spiritual food" in the five-month DTS. The first three months were a lecture phase, during which we learned topics such as the character and nature of God, hearing God's voice, faith and finances, evangelism, and the Holy Spirit. Twelve different topics were covered, and during that time I learned how to hear God's voice as never before. We had different speakers each week in the lecture phase, and these teachers wanted us not just to learn spiritual principles but to apply them in our lives.

The DTS students came from different cultures across Asia, so we were also learning from one another as we lived and worked together. The biggest lesson was how different cultures approached tasks and—in such diverse ways, with no culture being right or wrong!

I couldn't speak much English, so I struggled to communicate. I was always fearful that the speaker would ask me a question. Although I could understand the question, I didn't know how to answer or pray in English.

Carrie, my one-on-one staff leader from Canada, encouraged me daily. "Amongla, don't worry. It's okay to make a mistake. Just speak out what's on your heart." She prayed for me and spent lots of time helping me with the language.

After the lecture phase, we had another two months to go for evangelistic outreach, reaching out with the love of Jesus to unreached people groups, through various ministries.

When our staff divided us into teams and wrote our names on the blackboard for the outreach locations, I was unhappy because I wanted to go with the Nepal team. I wanted to see the place, and I wanted to go with my new friends.

Instead, they put me with the South India team. That very night when I was in a deep sleep on my upper bunk bed, I heard a voice saying, "Amongla, look at the wall." I saw written on it Romans 12: 1–2: "Therefore, I urge you, brothers in view of God's mercy, to offer your bodies as a living sacrifice, holy and pleasing to God—this is your spiritual act of worship. Do not conform any longer to the pattern of this world, but be transformed by the renewing of your mind. Then you will be able to test and approve what God's will is—his good, pleasing, and perfect will."

I quickly got up and wrote in my journal. When I fell back to sleep, the same voice told me, "That scripture is not only for you, but it is for your team members as well."

The next morning during my quiet time, God spoke to me that I was in the right team going to the right outreach location. That morning, I came to know the heart of God for my outreach location, and I asked forgiveness to God for my motives.

When we reached South India that night, most of us could not sleep. It seemed that something from the spirit world was disturbing our dreams, so I asked God what was going on. He showed me in a dream about a dark spiritual stronghold in the house where our team was staying.

The next day I shared it with our team, and we prayed. I also told our landlord about my dream. He said that a few months earlier a woman attempted to commit suicide in this house. To counter the spirit of death that lingered there, our team began to worship God and welcome his presence. As we sang songs and prayed over the house, the vexing spirit disappeared.

As we started sharing the gospel of Jesus in the villages and slums, people were healed. Others were set free from demon possession, and many others received Christ as saviour. We all experienced the anointing of the Holy Spirit; it was a fruitful and encouraging start for our team.

We visited a house where a man had been sick for many years and could not walk. Our team shared the love of Jesus, and we asked if he believed in Jesus. He said that he was raised as a unbeliever, but he believed in Jesus. We prayed for him, and he soon began to walk. He was so grateful, and all his family came to know Jesus.

Another time, we were singing and speaking to a crowd outside when a woman came to see what was happening. As we spoke, a demon caused her to tremble and roll her eyes. I prayed for her for nearly an hour before her big dark eyes opened, and she stared at me in wonder. The demon was gone, and she welcomed Jesus into her heart. We all experienced the presence of the Holy Spirit, and more than a thousand people were touched by the gospel during our two months of outreach.

DTS transformed my life. I was able to understand God's heart for the nations and began to discover His calling and destiny for my life. After completing the school program, I went back home—where I continued with my job to support my family as well as starting a four-year extension study for a Bachelor of Theology at the Working People's Bible College in Dimapur.

Since I am the oldest of five siblings, my parents expected me to support our family financially. I did, but after more than a year, I went back to Y Bangalore to serve as DTS staff.

Every Wednesday, our team went to different slums and villages to serve and pray for the poor and needy. We distributed clothes, toiletries, and food. We gave haircuts and showed people how to keep clean. Most importantly, we wanted to show them the love of Jesus through our words and deeds.

We sometimes travelled by bullock cart to the slums with Korean friends from the Bangalore base. The poverty and filth in the slums were some of the worst I'd ever seen. We set up a tent there and set to work caring for the people. One day, an elderly man with leprosy came for help. My stomach churned when I saw his wounds, but one of my friends and I cleaned them, and sent him on his way. The man returned each time we came, and his wounds and his heart began to heal. People with paralysis and various diseases came to ask us to pray for them. Many were healed instantly.

One morning, during my quiet time I sensed a disturbance in my spirit, and I wondered why. I asked God to show me but got no direction. After our community worship time, I went with Aunty Arina, who was the cook for our school, on her two-wheeler to the cantonment train station to book a train ticket for my return to Nagaland.

While Aunty Arina was driving, I felt scared. Military vehicles were racing down the crowded streets, and one of their motorcycles hit our motorbike. It spun us around, and we landed in a heap with more vehicles swerving to avoid us.

Arina's leg was bleeding, and I felt like an electric shock had hit my body. For a moment, I thought I was dying. When a policeman arrived, he asked who they should contact. I gave him my DTS leader Sandeep's contact number. I remember nothing about what happened after that, but I heard that Sandeep had rushed to the site of the accident and learned that we had been taken to the hospital.

Sandeep said I was unconscious when he got there. He called to me, and I opened my eyes. Then he said something I couldn't understand. I slipped back into unconsciousness. Aunty Arina was awake but in much pain from a bleeding and broken leg. Doctors sent her to another hospital to set the bone. I was also transferred to another hospital to be treated for a head injury.

Meanwhile, other Y staff were informed and rallied to help us. Sandeep went to the police station to get some compensation for medical expenses, but they refused to help. "I think the military personnel had bribed the police because in their report they made the accident look like it was the fault of Arina and Amongla," Sandeep explained.

The accident took place at about noon, but I wasn't seen by a doctor until 10 p.m. I was unconscious and lying on a stretcher for those ten hours. Finally, a doctor from Northeast India happened to see me in the hospital lobby and immediately ordered a brain scan. It showed bleeding in the brain. The Y staff were now praying intensely for both Arina and me. Hospital staff did another scan three days later and found no evidence of bleeding or swelling. It was a miracle!

Sadly, Arina's leg took months to heal. I kept wondering, why did this happen to us? Had I missed God's instruction? What if I died here, so far away from home? I felt shame and fear, but I wasn't going to let the forces of darkness defeat me. God was healing my brain. And, in one other miracle, all my hospital bills were paid by my Y family.

Once I felt well again, I headed back to Nagaland. I didn't know what I'd be doing next, but I was so grateful for God's healing and the support of my Christian friends.

Figure 2   My DTS class.

Chapter 4
Hearing God's Voice

As the new year began, I knew I needed to make a decision. I wanted to be involved in full-time ministry, but without a salary to cover my living costs and to help my family, I felt like I couldn't do it. Frustration over this decision was paralyzing me. How could I please God if I couldn't trust him for my financial needs?

I decided the only way to be sure of God's direction was to fast and ask him to guide my next steps.

I fasted for three days, full of expectation that God would speak to me. The first day God did not speak to me. The second day he was also silent. On the third, I pleaded with God to answer me.

As I was lying on my bed with my eyes closed, I saw a vision of a man wearing a white shirt. He came and sat beside me. He said, "Amongla, you should join Y." When I opened my eyes, he was gone, so I ignored it. Again, I heard him say, "Amongla, you should join Y." Again, I ignored it. The third time, the same audible voice said, "Amongla, you should join Y."

Though I knew the answer, I still asked, "Is that really you, God?"

I loved my work at Y, but I was afraid of living by faith. Y pays its workers no salaries. Each worker learns to trust God to meet their financial needs. I simply couldn't figure out how I could support myself and help my family if I didn't get a salary.

I tried applying to work at other Christian organizations, but no doors opened for me. I still had my job at the paper mill, but I did not have peace of mind.

One morning I woke up with the left side of my face paralyzed. I looked in the mirror and saw that even my left eye was not moving. I screamed, "What's happening to me?" I knew immediately that this affliction was linked to my refusal to follow God's direction, and I asked him for forgiveness.

My brother, Lanu, was now working as a doctor in Dimapur, so I decided to go see him. He and my cousin brother, Tali, were waiting for me at the bus station, and my brother took me to hospital for treatment. For a few weeks, I couldn't see much change. My prayer partner told me to keep trusting God for a miraculous healing. I did, and in a few weeks, God healed me completely.

God was confirming again—through my dreams and scripture, as well as through my prayer partners— that I was to join Y. I finally told my family, "I must go to join Y, I said "I will obey God rather than you. I'll have to give up my job."

"How are you going to survive without money?" my father demanded. "Who is going to support you financially? We can't help you, and you will die without food. Do not make this decision."

They even said, "Who will take care of your dead body if you die over there because of lack of food? Your dead body will be eaten by vultures" Even some of our relatives told me, "You are foolish!"

I understood their concern for my future, but I knew I had to obey God. The only one who encouraged me to obey God was my dad's sister, Onu Amenla. She knew I was called by God. She reminded me of the promise in Matthew 6:26: "Look at the birds of the air; they do not sow or reap or store away in barns, and yet your heavenly Father feeds them. Are you not much more valuable than they?"

Although I was ready to go, I was seeking God for the right timing. I was also praying for the location where God wanted me to go. One night I saw in my dream a map with a focus on south India. I woke up and wondered whether God wanted me to return to Bangalore.

Although I felt peace about it, I still wanted a second confirmation from the Lord. One week later, the postman came and gave me a letter. As I opened it, I knew I had my confirmation. It was an invitation letter from Y Bangalore base leader's wife, Chungme!

God was speaking to me from Genesis 12:1: "The Lord said to Abram, 'Leave your country, your people and your father's household and go to the land I will show you.'" I told my parents that was what I needed to do. "I believe that God will take care of me."

I left for Bangalore in January 2001. I knew it was the right choice, but on the four-day journey, I kept thinking about my family and worrying about my mom's health. Although she was doing so well now, her health had ups and downs. Being the oldest sister, I felt responsible for her.

While I was away, Y Bangalore moved to a new location on Ring Road. It was much larger and nicer than the Kamananahalli facility and was situated near a small park. The staff welcomed me warmly and gave me time to rest. A few of the staff members were from Nagaland like me. That made me feel even more accepted and welcome.

I had saved some money to help cover the cost of my room and food (1,200 rupees per month). When my savings ran out, I couldn't pay the staff fee on time. My leader reminded me that I needed to pay this by the deadline. I kept praying and trusting God. Though no money came in, a good friend from Manipur gave me a stylish new pair of sneakers. The next day I was wearing the new shoes, and my leader called me to the office. "Amongla, how can you afford these new shoes since you have debt on your staff fee?" I smiled and said, "I did not buy them, they were a blessing for me."

Another blessing came when several of us were given the opportunity to work at a new seven-star Hotel called Leela Palace near Bangalore Airport. The work involved housekeeping for which we were paid 20 rupees per hour. The work began at 4:30 each morning, and once completed we hurried back to the base for a full day of activities.

The money I earned was not enough to cover my fees, but the work taught me to be diligent and humble. In Y there is a saying, "Do the possible and God will do the impossible." That's what happened to me.

One afternoon in May, I heard the postman calling, and one of my friends said, "Amongla, there is a money order for you." I was so shocked as I couldn't think who would send money to me. I was even more shocked to learn that my brother had sent me 3,000 rupees. I never expected him to send money. I began praising God and thanking him for my brother as well.

Another day, I found 500 rupees under my pillow along with a tube of toothpaste. I still have no idea who put this under my pillow. On it was a note that said, "Blessings for you."

I took that money and went to the terrace, giving thanks to God. Then the Lord spoke to me, "Amongla, that money does not belong to you, give it away." He showed me two of my friends' faces, so I called them one by one and divided the 500 rupees between them. They had been praying for that exact amount, so they were overjoyed.

I learned that day that there's often much more joy and blessing in giving than in receiving.

Chapter 5
Hardship and Breakthrough

One Saturday night, I received a phone call from my brother saying our mother was seriously ill. He said that, from a medical perspective, there was no hope. This news hit me like a punch in the stomach, but I knew it wasn't the final word. My God can do miracles.

"Should I come home?" I asked.

"It's up to you," my brother replied.

"Let me pray about it."

I was not able to sleep that night. I felt so restless. The one thing I could do was to pray for my mum's healing and a long life. I decided to fast and pray until I got an answer from the Lord.

I prayed, "Lord, I committed my life to serve you. I left my home and family, but I don't want my mum to die now. Would you please heal her?"

Every night as my roommates slept, I went to the bathroom and knelt down crying and praying, sometimes as late as 2 a.m. After a week of this, I saw a vision of five chicks looking for their mother. Finally,

I found the chicks' mother in the jungle, and I brought her back to be reunited with her five chicks. When I opened my eyes, I asked the Lord, "What does this vision mean?"

"The five chicks are the five siblings in your family. Your mother is not going to die now."

Very early in the morning, I called my brother, and told him, "I will not come home now. God spoke to me that mum will not die now, he has answered our prayers." After this, I felt at peace and continued with my responsibilities, which included leading an outreach team.

That September, I prayed fervently for the Lord to show me where to take our team. A few days later, the name Salam came strongly to my mind. I thought that God was speaking to me. In my language that word means handshake, but in Hebrew it means peace.

When I asked a fellow staff member if he knew of a place called Salam, he said, "Yes, Amongla, there is such a place in South India."

Right away, he showed me the map and I was shocked. When God gave us confirmation, my school leader and I went to see the location and to meet a Y couple and a local pastor who was serving there. We sang for them a song God gave us about the people of

Salam. Whenever we sang that song, our eyes were filled with tears because we felt the presence of God.

In the last week of our lectures, speaker Mr. Jig taught on "Mission" and the importance of full commitment to God. He reminded us there will be times of trouble, times of hardship, and times of difficulty. Then he challenged us with this question: Are you willing to sacrifice your life for Jesus?

It was such a powerful teaching, and I declared to God that day, "I have decided to follow Jesus. There's no turning back."

Our team rode by bus from Bangalore to Salam where a local pastor welcomed us. He took us into his home, which had only one bedroom, a small kitchen, and a living room. Our team slept in the living room, in which we made a partition for men and women.

Shortly after we arrived, we asked, "Pastor, where is the bathroom?"

"We don't have one."

"Okay, where is the toilet?"

He replied, "We don't have one. You will need to dig a small hole out among the mango trees and do your business outside."

Our team looked a bit shocked, but we did what we had to do. We bathed wearing our old clothes and tried to defecate mostly at night. The funny part was sometimes as we were about to squat down in the dark, someone else would pipe up, "I am here." Since it was dark, we couldn't see if anyone was nearby.

The ministry time was very good. We walked from village to village, preaching in open-air settings and making house visits to tell people about the love of Jesus.

One morning while we were praying and reading scripture, some friends came to the pastor's house, searching for me. They said, "Amongla, did you read this morning's newspaper?"

"No, I've been here."

"You've surely heard about the new restrictions law."

"Yes, but what is your concern?"

"The eaders have declared that anyone who talks about other religions will be put in jail for fifty years and must pay a 50,000-rupee fine. Therefore, Amongla, we encourage you to take your team back to Bangalore."

I did not respond right away, but said, "Well, we will pray and see what God wants us to do." A few minutes later, our base leader called, saying, "Are you guys coming back? Some of our students' parents are calling me. They are afraid you will all be arrested."

I didn't know what to say. I couldn't understand how God could so clearly bring us here and now want us to leave. I called a team meeting, and we all agreed to fast and pray for three days. Our host pastor asked us not to use his house for our prayer times, and he helped us find a nearby location.

As we sat in a circle together, praying and waiting to hear God, I saw a vision. I saw the building collapsing. I asked God what it meant. He said, "Whatever government regulations they put in place will not harm you." And all the students said God spoke not to go back but to continue ministries.

It was clear God wanted us to continue his work there, so we told the pastor what we decided. He said, "If God spoke to you, then we will continue the work."

He then said, "From tomorrow onwards we will go on foot to the villages. That involves about four to five hours of walking. Is that okay for you guys?"

We all agreed and started walking right after breakfast. We often came back about 9 p.m. after sharing the gospel from village to village. Many people had never heard about Jesus, so we were able to tell them about the love of Jesus.

In one village, we sang a few songs and performed a drama called "Burden." Many people came to see us, curious about what was happening. While we were about to share the salvation message, I saw a man coming from the mountainside and listening to our message. Afterwards, we met individually with those who wanted to follow Jesus. I got an opportunity to speak to the man from the mountain. He said, "You know, I went to that mountain to commit suicide."

When I asked him why, he said, "I don't have any family, and no one loves me. I borrowed money to set up my farm, but this year there was no rain, so I am unable to pay the loan. I had no hope, so I felt it was better commit to suicide, but when I saw you singing songs so beautifully and I saw so many people here, I felt like I should come and see what is going on. As I was listening, I felt something different in my heart."

His face was streaming with tears, and he asked us where we were from. We told him we came from Bangalore to share the gospel. In the end, this man said he wanted to accept Jesus Christ as his personal saviour, and he received hope in a hopeless situation.

The next day as we were house visiting, we saw a lady standing alone in front of her house. We went to talk to her, and she said that she was about to burn herself alive. When we asked her why, she told us her husband was always drunk and beating her.

"It is too much for me, I cannot bear it any more. I have no peace. In my culture, once you are married you can't go back to your family, so I was about to burn myself." As we told her about the love of Jesus, she too accepted him as her personal saviour.

Another time while we were doing open-air ministry in a village, a woman in the crowd started shouting at us. It soon became clear that she was demon-possessed. The demon threw her to the ground, and she screamed and wailed and rolled in the dirt. Her eyes were ablaze with terror. We surrounded her and prayed for three hours until the demon left. "I feel peace," she said, as tears rolled down her face.

During our two months in Salam, we saw many similar wonders and miracles. A total of 245 people accepted Jesus Christ as their personal saviour, and we helped to start six churches in different locations. We handed over to our host pastor the care of the new churches. We thanked God for what he was doing in us and through us. We saw many confirmations during that outreach, that this was the plan of God for the outreach location. Although we faced many challenges, God protected our team. It was God who spoke to us to come to Salam, and we obeyed.

Another time, I took part in an outreach to Karnataka in south India. We visited house to house and were welcomed into the home of a family of another faith family. We told them about Jesus, and towards the end of our conversation, we asked them what we could pray for.

The wife said, "Here in our place, there has been no rain for the last three years. It is so hard, especially for the farmers. Please pray for rain, and if the rain comes after you pray, we will believe that your God is the truth, because even though we have been praying to our god, there's still no rain."

I replied, "Please understand, we are not God, but Jesus is. We will pray as you requested, but Jesus is the one who can do the miracle."

In my heart, I was quaking, but our team prayed in great faith. We left their house at about noon. By 6 p.m., dark clouds were rolling in, and the sky lit up with lightning, thunder, and heavy rain. We praised God for his miracle, and the next morning we returned to the same house. They were desperate to see us. When we entered, they said, "Your God is the true God. We want to accept Jesus Christ as our Lord." The whole family welcomed Jesus as their saviour!

Chapter 6
Outreach in Sri Lanka

In all my years of life, I had never been on an aeroplane and never been outside my native India. But that was all about to change. God was about to launch me on a new spiritual adventure that would require a deeper measure of faith.

In January 2003, as I was praying for an outreach location, I had a remarkable dream while serving on the Discipleship Training School (DTS) staff at Y Bangalore. In the dream, I saw a map of Sri Lanka, an island nation off the southeast coast of India. I woke up in the morning wondering whether this meant our DTS outreach team would be going there.

I was not convinced the dream was from God, so I did not share it with anyone. I just kept praying, "Lord if it is your will, please give me confirmation."

Two weeks later, a fellow staff member and I were making breakfast when he asked, "Amongla, are you praying for the upcoming outreach location?"

"Yes, I am. Why are you asking?"

"In my dream last night, I saw that you are going to Sri Lanka."

His words caused my heart to leap. This was the confirmation I had been praying for, but I did not tell him about my dream. I still wanted one more sign.

Each DTS is followed by a two-month ministry outreach. We typically ask students to pray about the outreach location. After praying one day, one of our students said, "God spoke to me to go to Sri Lanka." Another said the same, and of course, that was enough confirmation for me. I told our school leader how God has been speaking to me about Sri Lanka.

He said, "Amongla, if God is leading you this way, the challenge will be finances. We don't have money to go overseas, so you guys will have to trust God to provide the money you need."

Hebrews 11:1-3 says, "Now faith is being sure of what we hope for and certain of what we do not see. This is what the ancients were commended for. By faith, we understand that the universe was formed at God's command so that what is seen was not made out of what was visible."

Shortly afterwards, we divided into outreach teams, with six of us in the Sri Lanka team. Our team started fasting and praying for finances and for the right person to host us. We heard about one Sri Lankan pastor, and I began to communicate to him regarding hosting us and guiding us to ministry opportunities. Pastor Chandrasekaran had a small church, but he welcomed the opportunity to host our Y team.

As the outreach time approached, we didn't have enough money to book our flights or cover additional travel expenses. So, we prayed all the more. "Lord, if it is your will, please provide for us."

Other teams were leaving for different locations, but we waited for two more weeks for finances to come in. While we were waiting, we went to Mysore for two weeks of ministry, but our team members were growing discouraged. Two of them said, "We don't want to go for the Sri Lanka outreach; we don't want to deal with this kind of challenge." Their attitude was bringing disunity to the team, so I asked God what to do.

"Keep trusting me," he replied. So, I did. I kept telling the students, "God will make a way."

After two weeks, we still had no money to pay for our flights. But one day as I prayed, I felt led to call the travel agent. I didn't know him, but I said, "Sir, I need six tickets for Sri Lanka," and gave him the details.

He said, "Okay, when are you going to bring the money for the tickets?" I asked him where his office was and said, "I don't have money right now but, I will give it to you as soon as possible." I had a strong faith that God would provide.

The phone call was in the morning. That afternoon one of our friends was looking for me, "Amongla, this is for your team. Somebody gave it to me to pass on to you." I was shocked, wondering what this could be. I tore open the envelope and inside was the exact amount of money we needed for tickets for our team!

Inside was a letter from an international team that had visited our base. It said: "You blessed our team when we came to on outreach to Bangalore. God spoke to us to bless your team. I heard that your team needed funds for a trip outside the country." When I saw this big blessing, I wept with joy. I called all my team members and shared what we received. We gave thanks together to God for the miracle. We could now pay the travel agent in full.

We booked our tickets from Bangalore to Trivandrum by train and Trivandrum to Colombo by flight. Upon reaching Trivandrum, we stayed at a believer's house who lived near the beach. She was a poor woman, but she accommodated us overnight and gave us food out of what she had.

Early the next morning, we went to the airport and stood in the queue to check-in. As I handed my passport to the airline agent, he said, "Sorry, Madam, you cannot travel."

"Why not? I have a ticket."

"You and all your people require an immigration letter."

"I don't know anything about such a letter," I said. Since this was the first time first time flying and leaving the country, I was nervous to the point of tears. Our flight was about to leave, and I had no idea what we should do. I began to pray, asking God to help us and when I looked up there was an officer standing behind us.

I turned and pleaded, "Sir, can you help us? We are supposed to be flying today but we've been told we need an immigration letter."

"You cannot fly today since it is too late. But if you go to the immigration office and get your paperwork, I will try to help you get on a flight tomorrow."

Then he realized the immigration office was closed. Our hearts fell, but as we prayed at the airport, we all agreed to go by faith to the immigration office. When we reached the office, we saw the door had its shutter half-closed with an official just leaving. I ran and asked, "Sir, is the office open today?" He shook his head.

"No, I just came to pick up something."

I wasn't going to give up easily. "Sir, would you please consider helping us?" I explained our situation. He looked at me with a frown, and said, "Hurry." He gave us the forms, which we filled in within a few minutes.

I remembered God's word to us from Luke 18:27, "What is impossible with man is possible with God." We got our immigration letters.

We stayed again at the believer's house, but none of us could sleep. We just kept worshipping God and thanking him for his help.

Early the next day, we went to the airport, and we looked for the officer named Suresh who had offered to help us. When we met him, I asked, "Sir, is any seat available for us?" He said so far no. My heart was beating hard. What to do? We wouldn't stop praying. The departure time was imminent. We proclaimed, "Lord, we trust you."

Within a few minutes, Suresh returned and said to me, "Okay Madam. Just now five passengers have cancelled their flights, so you cannot go but the other five can."

"Oh no, Sir, I am leading the team, why can't I go? Sir, please."

He looked at me and smiled, "I am only joking. You guys are very lucky, it doesn't happen often, but just now six passengers cancelled. That means you all can go. Have a good day."

With tears in our eyes, we all boarded the flight to Colombo Airport in Sri Lanka. When we arrived, we were expecting the pastor to pick up us, but when we called him, he told us we would have to take a train to a place called Vavuniya, and that it might take about two and a half hours.

Yet another journey! We went by train to Vavuniya and were met by some church members. They picked us up and took us to meet the pastor, who lived near the church. Pastor Chandrasekaran asked whether we had any money for renting accommodation.

"We have a little money for food and transportation, but not for accommodation. We are trusting the Lord to meet our needs while we are here."

The pastor said, "Okay, then girls can stay in the church garage and the boys can sleep in the church."

That evening, the pastor gave us a big pot of rice and fish curry. After the meal, I went to take a bath. While I was bathing, a small frog jumped on my body. I shrieked so loud that two of my female friends came running.

"Are you okay, Amongla?" they asked.

"No, I'm not. There's a frog in here, could you please help me?"

My friends laughed, but they knew I was dead serious about getting rid of the frog. I have always been afraid of those slimy creatures. Unfortunately for me, Sri Lanka has a wet, cool climate that's perfect for breeding frogs and other reptiles! It's also a perfect climate for growing tea, and much of the world's tea is harvested there.

Forever after that, I've had friends check for frogs, snakes, and spiders before I take a bath in a new location.

The following day, we started our ministry times. Unlike India, Sri Lanka is a Buddhist country. We asked the Lord to give us specific strategies for presenting the gospel to the Sri Lankan people.

We woke up early each day and had some prayer time and fish curry before heading out for the day. We often went to rural villages, where we performed skits, sang songs, and preached about the redeeming power of Jesus. We went on foot from village to village, sometimes doing seven or eight open-air presentations a day. We returned by 10 p.m., after which we had dinner and a team debrief before sleeping.

Sometimes when we reached out our hands to pray for young people, the Holy Spirit would topple them to the ground. Their parents were worried until they saw their teenagers wake up full of joy and praising God.

Pastor Chandrasekaran was very happy with what he was hearing and helped us to get more contacts for the ministry.

On our way to our ministry time, we met a Christian woman who asked, "Where are you from?"

"We are from Y in Bangalore, India, and we came here to share the gospel."

She started crying and she said, "Two months ago, God spoke to me about a team coming from India and said that I should take care of them. From today onwards, I will provide food for your team." Again, we were amazed by God's faithfulness. As we ministered in people's houses, village streets, refugee camps and churches, many people accepted Jesus as their personal saviour. We were able to preach and minister the love of Jesus in four districts of Sri Lanka.

During the last week of outreach, we had a team meeting, and we were so encouraged by what God had done. At the end of a DTS outreach, we typically put on a love feast for the host family and translators. Unfortunately, this time we were not able to make them a special meal, but we made some simple dishes and honored them with thank-you cards and prayers.

Two days before we left for India, the pastor asked, "Amongla, do you guys have money to pay for your airport tax?"

He said the tax was 1,000 Sri Lankan rupees per person. "Oh, my goodness, we don't have that. What shall we do?" I gathered the team members and told them about the airport tax and began to pray for God's provision.

Just before our intended departure for India, we received an invitation for lunch from one of the families who used to support us on our outreaches. We had a special worship time together and prayed for their family. As we were leaving, they handed us an envelope. Inside was exactly the amount we needed for the airport tax—6,000 rupees! We had not shared with anyone that we needed money for the airport tax, but God uses people as a resource, and he is our provider.

Once again, I thought of Matthew 6:25–27 in which Jesus said, "Therefore I tell you, do not worry about your life, what you will eat or drink; or about your body, what you will wear. Is not life more important than food, and the body more important than clothes? Look at the birds of the air; they do not sow or reap or store away in barns, and yet your heavenly Father feeds them. Are you not much more valuable than they? Who of you by worrying can add a single hour to his life."

When we arrived at the Colombo airport and stood in queue to be checked in, the personnel informed us that we would be unable to travel today.

"Why not? We have our tickets."

"It is not your fault. The flight is overbooked, but don't worry, we will provide a hotel for you to stay in overnight."

We were taken to a five-star hotel, where the manager asked how many rooms we would need. We said six rooms, and we were each given a luxurious private room. It was a great ending for our walk of faith. After we had a rest and shower, we went downstairs to eat. There was much food to choose from and we thoroughly enjoyed ourselves. Afterwards, we went swimming in the massive hotel pool. As we played like rich tourists, I marvelled at how God blesses and honours us when we obey Him. We gave all glory to God.

The next morning after breakfast, a van picked us up to take us to the airport, and we left for India praising God for his faithfulness, his leading, and his favour. We returned to the base with great joy, honouring God for having met all our needs. "And my God will make all your needs according to his glorious riches in Christ Jesus" (Philippians 4:19).

Chapter 7
New City, New Faith Walk

When I first started staffing the DTS, people would ask me, "Amongla, what is your vision?" I said I didn't know for sure. I knew God had spoken to me about joining Y as a full-time Christian worker and I just obeyed him. So, I started asking God to reveal to me his specific direction for me. He said I was to "disciple and l the young."

I had counselling experience but had never taken a training course, so I prayed, "Lord, if it's your will, please open the door for me to attend a counselling school."

Some friends told me that there was an Introduction to Biblical Counseling course (IBC) starting at the University of the Nations campus in Lonavala. I was very excited to hear about the school, and I applied for it in faith. Now I had to trust God for my school fees and other needs. When I got an acceptance letter from the school leader, I knew the Lord was taking me into new territory—both physically and spiritually.

Lonavala sits in the mountains, northeast of the great Indian city of Mumbai. When I entered the campus, I was bowled over by the beauty of the surroundings. There were so many trees and gardens!

The Lonavala staff welcomed me and immediately made me feel like part of the campus family. By this time, I had been serving in for seven years, and I felt confident that I was in the place where God wanted me.

One of the greatest blessings for me was that I was now receiving ministry support in the amount of 700 rupees every two months through the India Adoption Plan started by YWAMers in the Netherlands. This was a huge help in paying my staff housing fees. I had no regular ministry support through my first years in the mission. Yet as I reflected on those years, I was amazed by all the ways God provided for me. He knows our needs, and he is absolutely faithful in providing for us.

Like the DTS, the counselling school is a five-month course, with three months of in-class training followed by two months of outreach. In class, I was astounded by how much I learned about my identity in Christ and how transformational this would be in my life. The school taught me how to handle emotional wounds from my past, how to receive forgiveness and healing, and how to use my own experiences to help others as a counsellor.

I learned to listen on a deeper level, both to people and to God. One of Y's Foundational Values is a commitment to hearing and obeying the voice of God. I wanted to hear his voice and stood eager to obey him. I was offered opportunities to serve in different capacities, but I made no commitments at that stage. I wanted to finish school and then seek God for what he wanted me to do after my IBC.

During the last week of our lecture phase, one of our speakers prophesied over each student. When my time came, he gave me these words:

"Amongla, the Lord says you are in a time where many things are changing in your life. Things are being created ... so that you have new influence and strength, new courage and vision. Father God is creating in your heart a strong gift to communicate, to understand and to express yourself, to teach. You have the discipline to help people to grow stronger and stronger. The Lord gave you a sensitive heart, thoughtful, very soft and gentle, with the patience to help people move ahead with strength.

"Father says you are a woman who takes time to build carefully and deeply because you want deep relationships and friendships. You want to fill in the gaps in your understanding, you want to experience things you haven't been able to before. God is going to create something fresh and powerful in you. He wants to surround you with new people and new understanding. Father wants to give you hope and understanding to bless other people.

"There is a whole new level of authority and responsibility that God wants to give to you. He wants to work in ways you haven't seen before. You will represent his love and truth to people, as a woman of influence who can help people to go through the process of change.

"So, continue the learning process; continue to allow old things to be cut off, and welcome the new direction, new relationships, and new opportunities God is giving to you. He says, 'I love you, Amongla, and I believe in you. Put arms around people and show them a mother's heart of love and compassion. Help them know healing love and be generous to them, allowing the expression of comfort to flow out of you … Amen.'"

That was an extremely encouraging and memorable word of encouragement for me. I started praying through these things with my prayer partner and my response to God was, "Lord, I am willing to go wherever you lead me."

Our class was divided into teams, which went to Nagaland, Kalimpong, Sikkim, and Bhutan. During the two months of outreach, we did teaching, counselling, case study research, and family life seminars.

During the outreach, I began to pray for my next step. God spoke to me about remaining at Y Lonavala. I came just for the school, but I was willing to stay on if that was God's will for my next step.

Right after I completed the counselling school, Lonavala's DTS school leader asked me to pray about co-leading their next DTS. As I prayed, I had the strong conviction and peace that this was God's will, so I said yes.

The school began with 35 students and seven staff, all of whom were eager to learn the ways of God and to practice them in a vibrant Christian community. But our joyful unity soon dissipated as the annual monsoon season pounded our training centre with relentless rain.

It became nearly impossible to do laundry as we could not dry our clothes. They soon began to smell of mould and fungus. Conditions were even worse for residents of the slums outside Lonavala. Their homes were built of wood scraps, cardboard, and other discarded building materials. Many of the homes collapsed in the rain, and residents were awash in mud and misery.

While we were out prayer walking, we came to a slum, and God spoke to us to start a ministry there.

Many of its people lived in tents, which were torn up by the storms. They were in desperate need of help.

At that time, police and political leaders were strictly controlling the activities of Christians in the area. We were not allowed to assist the slum dwellers or to share the gospel with them. But God made a way for us. We began to clean up the slum, sweeping the streets and distributing clothing to the poor.

The local political leaders finally granted us permission to do our cleaning work. The Slum residents had never swept their streets, so we showed them how to keep their community clean. We also collected money, bought them dustbins, and distributed them to each family. Over time, were we able to build relationships with the locals and teach songs and Bible stories to the children. One resident told us, "Whenever you come, we feel so happy and peaceful. Please come. You people are good."

People began to accept Jesus as their personal saviour; others were healed from different kinds of sickness.

One day, we visited the home of a 15-year-old girl who pleaded with us to pray for her. She said, "I have been sick for many months, and I am not getting better. I don't have a father. It's only me and my mum. When I went to the hospital, the doctor said I will die soon. I don't want to die now. Please pray for me so that I can live."

We asked her whether she believed in Jesus. She said, "Yes, I believe," and we shared the salvation message.

We visited her a week later, and she greeted us with a shining, happy face. We asked her what happened to her. She replied, "After you guys prayed, I was completely healed. I want to accept your God." That day she and her mother both received Jesus Christ as their personal saviour.

Because of growing political tension, we had to be careful about how we shared the gospel. Instead of praying in Jesus' name, we prayed to God.

I was leading outreach to Andhra Pradesh. As our outreach neared its end, God met our need for protection in a special way. Late one night, I had a dream and a voice called me two times. It said, "Amongla, leave this place right now."

I woke up wondering what had just happened. I began to pray, and within a few minutes, there was a knock at our door. The man who knocked told our host that we must leave immediately because the police were coming to arrest us for sharing the gospel.

I woke up all our people and we hurried to the train station, where we booked tickets to Hyderabad. Praise

God that we were able to stay in a mission compound there and finish our outreach.

What an outreach it was! So many people received healing and salvation and deliverance.

Chapter 8
Practicing Dependence on God

As 2006 began, I calculated that I needed a minimum of 3,000 rupees a month to cover my basic needs. I was tempted to tell others about this need, but I decided I first needed to fast and pray.

One of Y's Foundational Values is to Practice Dependence on God, and I needed to trust him more deeply at this juncture of my life and ministry. As I prayed, God moved in the hearts of a Brazilian couple to begin supporting my ministry with Rs. 500 per month for one year.

The Lord also spoke to me through Psalm 37:4, "Delight yourself in the LORD, and he will give you the desires of your heart." He soon began to give me new responsibilities with our upcoming school. I began processing student applications, asking God for a scripture promise for each student. I also called each applicant and their parents or pastor just to get to know them.

In July, we started the school program with nine staff and 31 students (17 males and 14 females) from different parts of India as well as from other nations.

God clearly had his hand on this class. One morning as we began to worship, all of us were filled by the Holy Spirit, we literally felt God's presence in our midst, and people began to speak in tongues. Some were crying, some were dancing, some were laughing. It was the most powerful spiritual experience I'd ever had.

We felt the presence of God like in Acts 2:1–4, "When the day of Pentecost came, they were all together in one place. Suddenly a sound like the blowing of a violent wind came from heaven and filled the whole house where they were sitting. They saw what seemed to be tongues of fire that separated and came to rest each of them. All of them were filled with the Holy Spirit and began to speak in other tongues as the Spirit enabled them."

Many lives were transformed in this school, and most of the students came back to staff DTS or to participate in other schools.

Although I was leading the school, I could not pay my staff housing fees on time. One day, our accountant called me in. She asked about my fee balance and said that those who could not pay their fees would need to leave the campus. When I came out of that office, I felt ashamed, and I began to cry out to God for help.

That very day, one leader of our campus called me. He said, "Amongla, my wife and I believe God is leading us to give you Rs. 1,000 per month." I was stunned and so thankful to them and to God. I began to weep, knowing I would no longer have to worry about my fees.

A few weeks later, the Lord gave me the extraordinary opportunity to serve for three days with Habitat for Humanity, a global non-profit housing organization working in local communities across 70 countries. Habitat envisions a world in which everyone has a good place to live. To our delight, a few of us from the Lonavala campus got to serve with former U.S. President Jimmy Carter, who was helping to build 100 houses in Lonavala, especially for the women.

When we went to the building site, it was full of security. As we entered the gate, we saw not only Jimmy Carter and his wife Rosalynn, but also actor John Abraham, and international cricket player Steve Waugh from Australia.

The houses were built with donated materials brought in from outside of India. It was a great experience for us, and with so many volunteers, the project was finished in about two weeks. All 100 homes were registered in the wife's name only. India's social system has treated many women like second-class citizens, and home ownership helped affirm the value of these women.

The following summer, God stirred in me a new level of faith after one of our speakers prayed for me. He said, "Amongla, God has called you in a very different way. God has anointed you, and people will listen whenever you speak. You are a woman of faith, and God is giving you a gift of mentoring and counselling."

Then some of my friends encouraged me to attend the Nations-to-Nations Leadership Training School (LTS) for three months in Amsterdam. The cost of attending such a school in Europe was staggering to me, but God kept bringing it back to my mind. So I kept asking Him, "Do I apply for this school or not?" I did not have a desire to go out of my country because I love India. But I realized it would be good for me to experience and understand other cultures.

I started praying, "If it is your will, please open the door for me to go. I will need lots of money for school fees, airline tickets, visas, and other expenses."

As I was seeking God, I had a dream. In the dream, I heard a voice say to me, "Amongla I will help you to go to the LTS in Amsterdam." I woke up in the morning, assured that God wanted me to apply for this school even though I didn't have money for it. I wanted more confirmation, so I asked Willie to pray for me. After he prayed for me, he gave me this prophetic word from Job 22:28: "What you decide on will be done, and light will shine on your ways."

I felt so encouraged, and I applied by faith. The application form mentioned that I should pay 50 euros for processing fees. How could I apply for this school if I didn't even have that amount? But I wrote to the registrar, saying I would pay when I arrived.

After a while, I had another dream. In this one, I received a parcel with a cup inside. The cup was printed with a picture of the Netherlands. In John 11:40, Jesus said, "Did I not tell you that if you believe, you would see the glory of God.?" He was clearly at work on my behalf because, after about two days, I received my acceptance letter. Soon, he did an even bigger miracle for me.

To process my visa, I needed 10,000 rupees, and I would have to travel to Pune to secure the visa. Once again, I asked God, "If it is your will for me to go, please provide for me. I trust you."

A few days later, I was in my room praying when I received a phone call. The voice on the other end said, "I came from Mumbai. I have something for you. Can you come now?"

I was thinking, "Who is this person?" I was a bit anxious about meeting a stranger, but I was curious. I went to look for him, and he was waiting with an umbrella in hand near the campus dining hall. He smiled when he greeted me and said, "This is for you from Pastor Willie in Mumbai." He handed me an envelope. I had never shared with Willie about my financial need, so I wasn't expecting a gift.

But when I got to my room I prayed and opened it, my heart nearly stopped. It was 10,000 rupees—exactly what I needed for my visa. I burst into tears of joy and began praising God. The next day I went to have the Pune travel agent process my visa, and I submitted the documents that were required.

The travel agent said, "You may need to go to Mumbai for your interview, so be ready."

After about two weeks the embassy called me for my interview, and they fixed my time early in the morning. Now I needed Rs. 1,800. I had Rs. 1,000 to book a car to the Mumbai embassy, but I needed 800 rupees more.

As I lay down, I bounced between feelings of faith and fear. I did not tell anyone of my need, but once again I cried out to God.

About 9 p.m., a friend knocked on my door. She said, "God spoke to me to give you 500 rupees since you are going to Mumbai tomorrow." Then, another friend came by and gave me another 300. I hugged them both and wept as I praised God for his goodness and faithfulness.

When my turn came, I went inside the Mumbai office, where an Indian woman asked me many questions. It was taking a long time, and I was getting anxious, but then I heard the Lord's voice: "Amongla, don't get upset, rather bless her." So, after the 45-minute interview, I said, "Madam, God bless you." And I left, confident that God was working on my behalf.

Two weeks later, when I was on a pastoral visit for a team in Bangalore, I received phone call from my travel agent, who said, "Madam, congratulations! You have been granted your visa." I had been so worried, but I shouldn't have. God and his promises never fail.

The next step for my trip to Amsterdam was to book my flight ticket. The price for a round-trip ticket was Rs. 40,268, way more money than I had. Then God spoke to me again from Philippians 4:19, "And my God will meet all your needs according to his glorious riches in Christ Jesus."

I asked my family to pray with me about my school in Amsterdam. After a week, several friends and family contributed towards my flight ticket, but I still needed another Rs. 33,000. This seemed like a big mountain for me. But I just kept asking God to provide, seeking him and believing in him.

On the morning of August 6, I was sitting in the reception area at our Lonavala campus, when one of the staff called me.

He said, "Amongla this is for you," and he handed me a thick envelope. I ran to my room and opened the flap. Inside was Rs. 33,000—the balance I needed for my ticket. God proved to me once again that he can and will provide for my needs whether large or small!

Chapter 9
A Future Arranged by God

Until that year (2008), my cross-cultural experience was mostly limited to South Asia, but the Nations-to-Nations Leadership Training School in Amsterdam changed all that. I was suddenly thrust into a First World nation and into a school with staff and students representing 45 nations.

It was exciting to imagine how God would knit together the hearts of such a diverse class. The first morning I went to the dining hall for breakfast, eager to meet some of the other students. It was clear that God brought me here because of all the financial miracles that opened the way for me.

However, the moment I looked at breakfast, I knew this new place was going to be a challenge. The menu consisted largely of eggs and cheese, with no rice—which was fundamental to our South Asian diet. I tried the new food, but I soon started vomiting and having loose motions. I was sick for two days. My friend Toshi from Nagaland bought me an energy drink, and after drinking that, I felt better. After about two weeks, I began to like the food, and our mealtimes allowed me to learn from people of other cultures.

We had 72 staff and students, and we all made adjustments in this cross-cultural blender of a school. My work duty was in the kitchen, where eight of us tried cooking food from a different country each night. It was fun, and it helped me to expand my worldview. People from cold climate cultures like Europe, and those from warm climates like South Asia have very different views related to individualistic and group activities, and it took time for me to understand.

Darlene Cunningham, wife of YWAM founder Loren Cunningham, came to speak at our school, and she introduced the image of a "belief tree." She explained how our beliefs are rooted in the values and practices of the culture we grew up in. She said God put beauty and value in every culture, and she challenged YWAMers to learn from them all. "They all bring glory to God, and they reflect his great creativity."

Throughout the school, we participated in activities that helped us to experience and celebrate the gifts of the cultures we represented.

Even our prayer times reflected our different cultural and religious experiences. Every Wednesday evening, we would go to "a house of prayer" led by a woman from YWAM Amsterdam. Our students loved interceding for this thriving international city and prayed intensely for people caught up in the city's sex trade. We also prayed for the country's leaders, schools, businesses, and families. I felt truly blessed to be interceding together for our host country, The Netherlands.

God was faithful to me during my time in Amsterdam. My school fees were 750 euros, and I didn't have that amount of income. God provided through sales of some handmade cards and jewelry I brought from India, from haircuts I gave, and from the gifts of a Dutch church where I was invited to speak.

In the LTS (Leadership Training School), I learned much about godly leadership, and I knew this season was a gift to prepare me for future ministry. I praise God for what I learned from the school's different speakers and from the young leaders around the world who were being trained. Loren and Darlene Cunningham and other senior YWAM leaders shared rich wisdom from the Word of God. Every day, I felt privileged to hear their stories, to discuss issues, and pray together.

I returned to India full of new zeal and purpose. I had a sense that God would be opening new doors for me. But I didn't have an idea about what that would mean until April of 2009 when a DTS speaker from Mumbai approached me.

He had been teaching about the Holy Spirit, and one morning he said, "Amongla, I would like to pray for you. I believe the Lord has an important message for you."

"Yes, please," I replied.

He reached out his hand and began to pray. Then suddenly he stopped and boldly spoke a prophetic word that would change the course of my life.

"Amongla, this year before October you will meet your life partner so prepare with fasting and prayer."

I looked at him with questioning eyes, but there was a certainty in his word that left me stunned. I went straight to my room and knelt beside my bed.

"Lord, how can this be? I don't even have a boyfriend."

But I did fast and pray, and I said to God, "If you want me to marry, I want to hear it directly from your voice."

Over the coming weeks, several people gave me scriptures that related to the word I had received about marriage. I still wanted more confirmation from God. The most direct word came from a visiting pastor who sat with me during lunch one day and said, "Amongla, I have a word for you. I sense strongly that three things soon will happen in your life:

1. You will meet your life partner, and you will begin preparing for your wedding in January 2010.
2. You will have a financial breakthrough.
3. A new season of fruitfulness is coming in your life.

Once again, the certainty in his voice left me convinced this would happen, but I longed for a word directly from the Lord. Once again, God was faithful, but the word came in a time and place I wasn't expecting.

Our DTS was divided into four outreach teams. I went to Nepal to set up for the arrival of our team at Kotak village, where we would be staying in a small and humble house.

One night as I slept, I heard a voice calling me. "Amongla, your life partner will be coming within three months."

I woke up suddenly and thought, *Who is calling me?* It was a loud, clear voice. I looked at my watch, and it was 3 a.m. I shook my head and went off to sleep again. This time I heard the same voice only louder. It said, "This is your confirmation!"

Immediately, I wrote it down in my journal, and the next morning I shared it with my friend. Her response was, "Okay, let's see what will happen. If this is God, it will come to pass soon."

"Yes, soon," I replied. That made me even more anxious about meeting this mystery man who God was preparing for me. How will that happen, Lord? How will I know?

I finished my work in Nepal and visited another team in Punjab. Still no mystery man. My next pastoral visit was to Thailand. That went well too, but still no marriage partner. On my return, I stopped in Kolkata to visit friends serving at the Y base. As we were sitting at the mission house the next day, a young man I didn't recognize came into the living room.

My friend Ayangla introduced us, saying, "Amongla, this is Tai. He's from Samoa, and he's here working with our DTS and with our ministry to street children."

I greeted him with a simple hello, and Tai shot me a winsome glance that took me by surprise. He had black hair, a round brown face, and a muscular build. He was wearing a chain necklace.

"Tai, Good to meet you."

He dipped his head and said, "We all are serving our living God." Then he left the room, and I tried to resume the conversation with my friends. Instead, they wanted to talk about Tai.

"Well, what do you think? Do you like him?"

"I don't know. He is a stranger to me."

"Well, God said he's sending you a marriage partner. Why don't you pray to see if he's the one."

"How can I marry someone I don't know? Someone who is a stranger to me. And he's from a different culture."

My friends could tell by looking at my face that I wasn't excited about their matchmaking efforts.

"Amongla, don't be proud. Give God a chance here."

"I will, but God will have to do it."

I came back from Kolkata to Lonavala by train, and after a few days, I received a phone call from my friend Ayangla in Kolkata. She said, "Amongla, I told Tai to pray for you—to see if it is God's will for you guys to marry."

It seemed strange for my friend to make such a request, but with so many words about marriage coming from various sources, I knew I had to take this seriously. I told my leaders in Lonavala and my parents what happened, and I asked them to pray for us.

One morning during my quiet time, God said to me, "Amongla, I have been speaking to you about this person."

On the evening of August 31, I received a phone call. "Hello Amongla, this is Tai in Kolkata. I have been praying for you. I know this may sound strange to you, but God spoke to me that you will be my wife. I know we don't yet know one another, but if it is God's will, he will bring us together. I will wait for your response."

I didn't know how to reply so I said, "Can you pray for two more weeks? I will pray as well, and whatever God says to us we should follow. Are you willing to wait for this confirmation?"

"Yes, I will pray, and I will call you in two weeks."

God spoke to Tai through Ecclesiastes 4:9. "Two are better than one because they have good return for their work." Best of all, God gave me peace to make the decision to marry him without knowing him personally. We trusted the Lord together in this, and we both believed he brought us together.

From the beginning, we processed our plans with our family, our leaders, and our prayer partners. All were very supportive and positive.

I decided to go to Nagaland for Christmas, and on my way, I stayed for a night at the Kolkata base. That evening they were having a Christmas program, and afterwards, they called Tai and me up front. The staff all surrounded us and prayed for us, so we had a surprise engagement party. That night, Tai gave me a silver engagement ring.

While I was in Nagaland for Christmas and New Year, Tai and I talked regularly by phone. Those calls helped me get to know this man whose name is Tai Setefano. He was born into a nominal Christian family of eight children and raised in Vaiusu, a village on the Samoan island of Upolu.

Later he shifted to American Samoa where he went to Bible college. Staff and students there were participating in a "Samoa for Missions" event, and the main speaker was YWAM's founder, Loren Cunningham.

"Loren's message inspired me," said Tai. "He encouraged us to pray about going to the nations. When I prayed, God put India on my heart." Tai later made a connection with Samoan YWAM leader Silo Schmidt, who was working in Bangladesh. He invited Tai to come there for a DTS, and he served there for a few months afterwards. When his visa expired, Silo encouraged Tai to move to Kolkata to join its street children's ministry.

Some of the things I learned about my future husband were that he was a man of deep faith and a great encourager. He was also quite introverted, which sometimes made for long silences in our conversations. After conferring with our parents and leaders, we fixed our wedding on March 4, 2010.

The Lonavala leaders encouraged Tai to come to Lonavala so we could serve together and get to know each other more deeply. That's what we planned—

until I received a phone call from Tai that shook us both. He said, "Amongla, did you read in this morning's newspaper about the new law that requires all the foreigners living in India to go out of the country for two months to renew their visas?"

"No, I haven't heard about this. What are you going to do?"

"I plan to go to Nepal since it is closest, but I feel like the Lord wants to get me back here quicker than two months."

"I sure hope so. If you can't get a visa, we won't be able to do the wedding as planned."

While Tai was in Nepal, I stayed in Nagaland and asked various friends to pray for the release of his visa.

One morning while Tai was in Nepal, I woke up with the distinct impression that he would be returning in two weeks. How was that even possible? I wondered, given the new government rule?

I prayed and fasted anyway. The very next day, Tai called to say he was going to the Nepal border to try to secure his visa. A few hours later he called from the visa office.

"Amongla, please pray! I'm standing in the queue with more than thirty people in front of me. Many people have had their applications rejected. I need you to pray that our Lord Jesus will grant my visa."

I prayed for Tai over the phone, and when his turn came, a man from another side of the office walked over and took his passport. He stamped "Approved," on the visa form, smiled at Tai, and said, "Have a good day."

Tai was shocked. He got his visa in two weeks instead of two months. A true miracle!

Once we were together in Lonavala, we started our pre-marriage counselling. It became a new adventure of discovery in getting to know each other and the cultures we came from.

Since neither of us had regular financial support, we planned a small wedding. I sewed my own simple wedding gown, and we bought a wedding outfit for Tai.

One of our DTS speakers asked me where we were going for a honeymoon.

"We don't have a plan," I replied, not wishing to mention that we had no money for a honeymoon. "Then come for three days to Goa," she said. "I will book the hotel for you guys." I was surprised and delighted. This would be such a treat, and we really needed more time to get to know one another.

One day I noticed Tai was not talking to me. Finally, he said, "You need to remember that we are already married in God's eyes. But you are making plans about our wedding and not including me in the decisions."

I was cut to the heart. "You are right, and I am so sorry. I promise not to move ahead with any wedding plans until I discuss them with you."

Tai smiled and accepted my promise. We decided to meet every week to talk about how we were doing in our communication. These meetings addressed our strengths and weaknesses, and they proved very helpful in our planning. We later reduced the number of meetings to once a month and then to once a quarter as our communication and our relationship grew stronger. God was indeed giving us one heart.

Chapter 10
A New Life Together

About 150 friends and family members attended our wedding on March 4th at a small resort in Lonavala. It was a simple yet meaningful ceremony. God had told me that my wedding would be before April. And it was. When God speaks, it is truth.

I was now Mrs. Setefano, and we soon set off for Goa on the honeymoon trip our friend had arranged. Our coworkers assumed this time would be all love and joy for us, but it was not like that. We are from different cultures, with different personalities, opinions, and expectations. We struggled in the beginning, but our marriage communication meetings really helped. We began each communication evaluation with an affirmation and then shared about areas where we wanted to see improvement. By God's grace, we saw progress every month.

Upon returning to Lonavala, we each resumed our ministry roles. I continued to lead the Discipleship Training School, and Tai served in the Regional Records Office. We stayed on campus in a tiny room for about four years after we married.

Our greatest need was for a refrigerator, so Tai and I prayed for one. We did not tell anyone but God of our need. A week later, a friend said to us, "I want you guys to get a small refrigerator so here is Rs. 2,500 toward that. We continued to pray, and a week later, another friend came to our room. He gave us Rs. 2,000. The next day someone gave us Rs. 500. We thanked God because when we went shopping, we found an 80-litre refrigerator we could afford to buy.

In 2010, our base leader asked me for a third time to consider joining the campus leadership team. I had refused two previous times because I didn't have a clear direction from the Lord. I wanted to hear his voice before making such an important decision. I told him, "We will pray and let you know how God is leading us on this decision."

One week later, during my quiet time, God spoke to me about the time recorded in 1 Samuel 9 when Samuel anointed Saul. I told Tai, "As I was meditating on this passage, I felt strongly that this is the right time, it is God's timing for me."

"I agree. I think this is the time. It's a new season of your life, and I'm confident you will do well."

"Thank you, dear husband," I said, reaching out to clutch his hand. "It's time to follow the Lord in this."

Tai wanted very much to return to American Samoa to introduce his new bride to his family. We began praying together about the timing of such a trip and for finances to purchase tickets. But we got no clear direction, so that Christmas we went to Nagaland to visit my family. It was the first time my parents met Tai, and they welcomed him like a true family member. He endured some culture shock experiencing life in a rural northeast east of village, but he did his best to fit in.

A few weeks after we returned to Lonavala, I started having severe pain in my stomach. I asked Tai, "What should we do?".

His face looked heavy with concern. "We don't have a good hospital in Lonavala. I think we should go to Pune for you to be checked at the hospital there."

In Pune, I was diagnosed with an ovarian cyst, and the doctor advised me to have it removed surgically. We agreed that I needed surgery but had no idea how we would pay our hospital bill.

One morning, my husband and I were praying about what to do, and an elderly woman from America who was visiting our campus greeted us. She came to our room, and we offered her coffee. As we began to talk, she asked about our ministry. She said, "I felt like God wanted me to bless you guys." She then handed us a cheque for $500 US (about Rs. 30,000). We were stunned at the way our faithful God met our needs.

My surgery took about two hours, and I stayed at the hospital for about one week. The hospital bill came out to Rs. 40,000. My surgeon is a Christian, and he said to us, "Amongla and Tai, give me only Rs. 35,000. "I will discount Rs. 5,000."

I said, "Oh sir, right now we have only Rs. 30,000 cash in hand."

"That's okay. Your life is more important than money. The remaining balance you can give me in instalment payments." It was another miracle, and I was discharged from the hospital soon after.

As we were thanking God, a few scriptures came to mind, including Psalm 46:10, "Be still, and know that I am God; I will be exalted among the Nations; I will be exalted in the earth."

What a joy to serve our living God, he is always faithful!

I was working under Ron and Bonny when they handed over their responsibilities to me, and the entire Lonavala community prayed for my appointment as DTS coordinator. Afterwards, international leader Lis C. encouraged me to do a professional coaching course. I did not take it seriously until Loren, one of the leaders also encouraged me to do an international professional coaching course. By the grace of God, I was able to do a two-year course and be certified as a trainer. It was a big boost for my confidence in leading the ministry.

When I started at Lonavala, we were running two Discipleship Training Schools a year at the campus. As I began to coach and mentor more DTS leaders, we were able to offer the DTS four times a year. We were now attracting over 100 students a year, including some from outside of India. We also began offering other schools, encouraging students to pursue their passion and vision.

In my new role, I was privileged to travel throughout India and occasionally abroad to do leadership development training for DTS programs. In all my training sessions, my goal is to impart whole-hearted devotion to the Lord.

The most joyful moment for me in any leadership course is when I see a student's transformation. As they grow in faith and obedience, their life changes. It reflects new spiritual maturity, and I see the abundant fruit of this in the students they serve. It is not easy to disciple and equip young people, but I know this is my calling and passion, and I love it.

I also love to visit my students serving in the mission field. Many are becoming better than me in their ability to teach and disciple others. I see them pioneering new ministries and being used by God in miraculous ways. I try to continue support of their lives through my prayers and encouragement, and I thank God for keeping us connected.

A doorway into a Muslim neighbourhood

As our student enrollment grew, we were faced with a new problem. We and other staff would have to find off-campus housing. Lonavala is a small city in the mountains near Mumbai and, because it attracts tourists, rents are higher than in other regions.

Tai and I began to search for a place to rent, but we found them to be very expensive. One day while out searching, we visited the home of some friends who lived in an old house, which had an empty downstairs area. We learned that the downstairs was used by a Muslim housing society on rare occasions. We asked if the landlord would allow us to rent it.

Our friend said, "The landlord lives in Mumbai, and she keeps it open for times when she visits Lonavala. But we've never seen her use it."

"Well, we really want to rent this place," Tai said. "It's not far from the market and just a 40-minute walk from the base. Because it's in a Muslim area, I think God will use us here."

We prayed right then that the landlord would allow us to rent it. We continued praying over the next two weeks and then called her to make our request. Finally, she agreed to let us rent it for Rs. 7,000 per month. Another miracle.

Our new landlord was a rich and influential Muslim. Many Lonavala Muslims were not happy with her when they learned that she had rented her flat in the Muslim Society space to a Christian couple.

She got calls demanding to know, "Why are you allowing Christians to stay in our society? Please do not allow this. We don't want to mix with people of other religions."

Thankfully, our landlord allowed us to stay, and we made a house agreement. She said, "Be careful what you cook and eat. Do not eat pork, and don't make noise. If you do that, I think there will not be complaints from the neighbours." We agreed to follow her guidelines.

Once again, we had to trust God for rent as well as for transportation and food. We had no bed. We had only our suitcases, a few clothes, dishes, and a three-litre rice cooker.

One day my friend, visited our house and he asked, "Where is your bed?"

"We don't have one. We are sleeping on the floor."

The next day, my friend gave us Rs. 10,000 to buy a bed. Right away, Tai and I went out and bought a beautiful double bed. As we brought it home, I thought of Matthew 6:8, in which Jesus says, "Do not be like them, for your Father knows what you need before you ask him."

My husband and I started to pray about how to reach out to our Muslim neighbours with the gospel. God said, "Make friendships." So slowly and intentionally we began smiling, greeting, and conversing with our neighbours. Whenever they did social work projects, we joined them. Every morning, Tai watered plants at the Muslim society's park. They always seemed grateful for our help.

During the summer, our campus has an abundance of jackfruits. We brought some home to distribute to our neighbours. This made them happy to have us in their neighbourhood, and they began to share some sweets with us during their festivals.

Every evening, I walked around the Muslim society area seven times, praying for them and their salvation as I went. One Muslim woman began to share her life story and her family struggles with me. It allowed me to share the love of Jesus with her. I prayed for her, and now whenever she sees me, she asks me to pray for her and her family.

One elderly neighbour suddenly became paralysed and was hospitalized. We asked her husband if we could visit her at the hospital. He said yes, and we began stopping by to encourage and pray for her. It seemed like every day God opened new opportunities for us to help our neighbours and show them the love of Jesus. God was clearly at work, enabling us to build relationships with them.

One neighbour told us he notices when we are away on a trip. "If you guys are not around, we don't feel good."

Even our landlord was happy with us. Whenever she came to Lonavala, she stayed with us and ate with us. She asked us to pray for her, and we were able to share the gospel. She said as we parted, "I love you guys."

Figure 2. Our wedding

Figure 3. Mr. and Mrs. Setefano

Chapter 11
Welcome to the Islands

My husband loved the people of India, and he was always doing things to bless them. But he missed his Pacific Island homeland and wanted me to meet his family. The cost of the airfare made it seem like an impossible dream, but we knew very well that nothing was impossible with God.

Tai and I had started praying for direction about a Samoa trip when we got a visit from my previous leader, Chungme from Bangalore. She asked, "When are you guys are planning to go to Samoa to visit Tai's family?" I told her we were praying about it.

"You need to plant seeds of faith," she said. "Here is the first seed."

Chungme handed me a US $5 bill. We put it in an envelope marked Samoa, and she began to pray over it. "Lord, please multiply this money so that Tai and Amongla can travel to Samoa and minister there. We remember your words in Mark 9:23 that "Everything is possible for him who believes."

Tai and I added to the envelope whenever extra money came in, and we asked God every week to multiply what we had. Soon, he began to multiply the amount in remarkable ways. Our travel agent in Pune told us that the cost would be Rs. 90,760 for each ticket. That was a huge amount for us, but we never gave up our trust in God. Every day we spoke positive words about the money coming in.

Friends gave generously to help us, and we also made and sold pickles to generate income. After two years of praying, God blessed us with enough money to book our flights. We were so excited, and we praised God daily for his provision.

We left for Samoa in December 2013 on what proved to be the longest journey of my life. We flew from Mumbai to Singapore, where we had a ten-hour layover. From there we travelled to New Zealand, where we stopped for another six hours, and then on Apia, the capital of Samoa. YWAM friends came to welcome us at the airport, and we rested for two days to recover from jet lag.

From Apia, we flew in a much smaller plane to American Samoa, where Pastor Asua Fuimaono and his wife, Della, were waiting. As we stepped off the plane, I heard wonderful Island music greeting the passengers.

Even sweeter was the scent of tropical flowers and the pure ocean air. I had seen the ocean before but never was it so blue as this.

While Tai was in Bible college, he had lived with the Fuimaono's. They welcomed us warmly and drove us to their home in a big car. They arranged for us to stay with them for the next two months. In their home, I learned so much about the Samoan culture, and it helped me to understand my husband better. It is a beautiful culture, and I deeply admire their warmth and hospitality. Coming from India where the food is rich with spices, I struggled with the simple island fare, but I soon began to like it. Samoans typically don't eat much rice, but as a blessing for me, they bought me a bag of rice. This made me feel so good and special.

During our stay there, we had opportunities to visit different churches to do ministry. The founder of "Samoa for Missions" gave us an opportunity to minister in schools and prisons, as well as to appear on radio and television. It was an amazing opportunity to share the love of Jesus in ways I'd never done before. We taught on the topics of evangelism and missions. We also helped to start an evangelism team at Antioch Church.

We launched a hospital ministry too. Whenever we visited patients, we gave them food and toiletries. We told them about the love of Jesus, and many people were healed both physically and emotionally. It blessed us that the people responded so well to our message.

Every day, I was deeply touched by the kindness and the hospitality of the Samoan believers. They honoured us for our work in India and treated us with incredible generosity. I felt privileged to have married into such a beautiful culture. Fishing is a big part of that culture, and the Samoans treated us to the best seafood I've ever eaten. Our more than two months in the country were a rich time of family, ministry, and new experiences.

God's favour was upon us through our whole time in Samoa. On our return home, we stayed for a few days at the YWAM base in Apia. I led some staff training sessions there, and it proved to be a great way to get to know the Samoan YWAMers.

The biggest surprise of our visit came after we returned to Lonavala. Some American Samoan churches had taken up a collection for us and sent a financial gift that enabled us to buy a used Maruti Suzuki car for our transportation. What a great blessing! We felt overwhelmed by this kindness, and we praised God.

Our new addition

Before I was married, God spoke to me one morning through a scripture that came to have a special meaning for us. It is a reminder of one of the first promises God fulfilled. After surviving the great flood that was God's judgment on the earth, Noah and his family made a burnt offering to the Lord.

Genesis 8:21 says, "The Lord smelled the pleasing aroma and said in his heart, 'Never again will I curse the ground because of man, even though every inclination of his heart is evil from childhood. And never again will I destroy all living creatures, as I have done.'"

This scripture was a prophetic word that God gave to me, "Lord, if I get married and you bless me with a baby girl, I want to name her Aroma." I prayed to God.

Only after about nine years of having said this prayer, God blessed me with a wonderful husband, and after about two years of marriage, he blessed us with our daughter. Aroma Setefano is God's special gift to us. She has a bright smile and dark flashing eyes that remind me daily of the blessings of our good Father.

On the first day of each new year, Tai and I prayed and fasted to seek God's direction. We would make a list of prayer points for the year, then in late December see how many prayers God answered. We were always amazed at his responses to our prayers.

January 1, 2016, started in the same way. As we prayed, God impressed on us a Scripture, Mark 11:24: "Therefore I tell you, whatever you ask for in prayer, believe that you have received it, and it will be yours." We didn't know how God would apply that verse, but we were confident in his faithfulness.

The big test came a few months later. Tai came home, and I could tell from the look on his face that he was anxious about something.

"You seem upset," I said, "What's going on?"

"You know my passport is expiring in September. I was hoping I could get it renewed here in India, but I learned today that I must go back to Samoa to do that."

"Oh, no." I felt like a great weight just landed on us. Tai returning to Samoa would be a huge expense for us. Our daughter, Aroma, was two and a half years old at that time.

"We need to pray," he said.

We prayed often over the next few months, and God reminded us of the Word He gave us in Mark 11:24. We prayed that all of us would be able to return to Samoa. We wanted Tai's parents to meet their new grandchild, and we began to ask that God would use us to strengthen his church in Samoa.

The ticket cost for the three of us seemed like an impossible burden. At times when we were most discouraged, God reminded us of the words of Jesus in Luke 18:27. "What is impossible with men is possible with God."

We did not share with people how much we needed for the tickets, but we fasted and prayed. Unexpected gifts began to come through friends in India and the Samoa church. Once again, God's provision was miraculous. Tai reminded me, "God knows when to bless, and how much to bless. He is always faithful."

We travelled to American Samoa and stayed there for nearly six months. By the grace of God, we not only did church ministries but also preached on radio, on television, and at the Bible college as well.

We also continued to encourage the evangelism team at Antioch church. We often joined them for outreaches in the community, demonstrating how to share the love of Jesus with people we met. Some of those people accepted Jesus Christ as their personal saviour, and others received physical and emotional healing as we prayed for them. As God led us, we did family counselling, prison ministry, youth meetings, home fellowships, and coached people. Every day was a new adventure in faith.

Our time in Samoa was a blessing for us and our daughter. I loved these island people. They were so kind and hospitable. I thanked God often for their generosity. We didn't deserve such overflowing kindness, but the Lord showered us with his grace.

Best of all, my husband was able to renew his passport. We returned to India full of joy and continued our ministry responsibilities at the Lonavala campus. It was refreshing and faith-building season for us. What did God have for us next?

Figure 4. Our family in 2023

Chapter 12
On to England

It felt good to be in India, serving with various ministries at the Lonavala base. But after a few years, I sensed something stirring in Tai's heart, and one day he finally addressed it with me.

"Amongla, what do you think about us going to out of the country to take the School of Biblical Studies (SBS)?" He wanted to rejuvenate as well as to have new experiences.

"Alright, let's pray to see where God leads us." The thought of how much such a trip would cost was overwhelming. However, I'd witnessed God's provision for us numerous times.

"If it's God's will for us, I know he will provide for us," I said. "I think it is his will, and I'd like us to pray about applying to SBS in the UK. The question is which one since there are more than one in the UK."

We started praying about the decision together. We saw it as an opportunity to learn God's word, have a break from our responsibilities in Lonavala, and learn from other cultures.

After months of waiting, we applied in January 2018 to the SBS at King's Lodge in Nuneaton, England. After receiving our acceptance, we applied for visas. We applied together as a family, but my 4-year-old daughter and I were granted visas before my husband received his. We applied a second time, and finally, we all received our visas.

The biggest challenge was the cost of the tickets. Once again, we started proclaiming God's promises and trusting Him for a miracle. As money began to come in from various sources, we thanked God every day. He provided just what we needed. As it says in 2 Corinthians 9:8, "And God is able to make all grace abound to you, so that in all things at all times, having all that you need, you will abound in every good work."

September 26, 2018

We left India on this day, and we arrived at the Birmingham, England, airport the following night. Two YWAM staff were waiting to pick us up and drive us to the King's Lodge campus, about 30 minutes away.

The enormous King's Lodge is set in lovely gardens with apple trees that we were allowed to pluck and savour. Once more, we had trouble adjusting to the food and way of life in Britain. Aroma was begging for some curry and rice, but the base kitchen had just some salad, bread, and cheese.

The base is home to people of many cultures. We started the process of adapting to these new people and to a new environment, which was so different from our homelands of India and Samoa. I observed that British culture is more task-oriented than our relational "warm climate" cultures, but each has its strength.

Tai started the School of Biblical Studies with great excitement, but the school required a heavy study load, and sometimes he got only a few hours of sleep. Even so, I could see the joy on his face as he went deeper into the Word of God. SBS was not easy for him, but he received a lot of encouragement from the staff and his classmates.

In the beginning, I struggled with this new environment, and I felt lonely. People didn't seem friendly. I guess they were too busy with their own business. I began thinking, *How can I survive like this for nine months? My husband is busy with his school, and hopefully, our daughter will be in school soon. What will I do then?*

Two weeks later, God connected me with a lovely Asian woman who lived next door to us.

"Hi, I am Yvonne. I am serving here, and I thought we should meet each other."

Yvonne's beautiful smile warmed my heart and gave me hope that I could one day feel at home here. As we sat there sipping tea, she said, "Amongla, please tell me your testimony. How did you meet Jesus? And what led you to YWAM?"

As I began telling my story, she also talked about her spiritual journey. At the end of our conversation, she said, "Can we be prayer partners?"

"Oh yes, I would love that. Let's pray for each other right now."

One day, Yvonne asked me for a list of our family members. So I asked why.

"Amongla, I have a friend in China who is a great prayer partner. Her name is Yanglirong. She is a committed Christian who loves prayer. I told her about you and Tai, and she wants to pray for you and your family."

Yvonne gave me her friend's contact information. After we started communicating, Yanglirong surprised us by sending 20 pounds per month to support our ministry.

There were nearly 10 of us from Asia living at King's Lodge. We all love to eat rice, so I asked the kitchen manager if I could help cook and requested that we serve rice twice a week.

She said, "That's very kind of you to offer, but you can't cook in a public kitchen unless you have taken a government course. According to UK law, you need to certify that you know health and safety rules before you can cook for the community. The government will come and check from time to time, even testing the food to see if it's served at the right temperature."

"I don't mind taking the training, especially if it helps provide food choices for the Asian people at the base."

"Okay, then. You can do the training through an online course."

After I finished the course, I was given a final exam. I scored 100 percent on it, and soon received my certificate. The base had several teams working in the kitchen, and I soon began to lead a team that made Indian food twice a week for the dinner meal. People loved it. Even those who lived off campus would sign up for meals whenever they heard that we were cooking yummy Indian food.

Living in the UK was super expensive for us. Just taking a bus into town cost about Rs. 500 in Indian currency. If we walked, it took about 45 minutes, so I decided to walk whenever I needed to go into Nuneaton. I prayed for the people of the city as I walked, and God gave me a new love for the people of Nuneaton.

In October, Aroma was admitted to the Milby Nursery. The school was free, and we decided to enrol her for a class that met only three times in a week, in the afternoons. It was a 20-minute walk to the school, and one day as I was dropping my daughter off at school, I saw a woman in front of the school, who appeared to be Indian. She also was dropping off her daughter. I kept looking at her, and she seemed warm and kind, so I walked over to meet her.

"Hello, I am Amongla from India, where are you from?"

She flashed a big smile and said, "I'm Debti. I am originally from Gujarat in India, but my family now lives in the UK."

"I'm pleased to meet you. My family arrived here just a few weeks ago, and now my husband and daughter are both enrolled in school."

She glanced at my clothes and said, "Here in England, the weather is very cold. Do you have warm clothes?"

"No, this cold weather is new for us."

"I would like to give you a warm jumper, where do you live? I will bring it tomorrow."

"Wow, that's very kind of you. We live at King's Lodge here in Nuneaton."

The next day she brought some warm jumpers for me and some toys and books for Aroma. As we got to know one another, I learned that she was from a prominent family. Her husband is a medical doctor, and she has two kids, a boy and a girl. We became good friends. I asked questions about her religion and also shared my testimony about faith in Jesus.

Whenever my husband was free, he walked with us to Aroma's school. Along the way, we asked God to use us to bless this community. He did so by introducing us to a schoolteacher named Mary and other believers from New Life Church.

Mary said, "We used to go for evangelism on weekends, but that stopped some time ago. We'd like to do it again. If you are willing, let's go together every Saturday."

We were willing. So, every Saturday we went into Nuneaton to share the gospel, listen to our neighbours' stories, offer food and coffee, pray for people, and show the love of Jesus in other ways.

One guy we prayed for was paralyzed in half of his body. He got healed, and he began to believe in Jesus. Another person got a job after we prayed for him. We introduced him to a nearby church, and he soon began attending. I encouraged friends in YWAM to join us for evangelism, and slowly more friends participated in our weekend outreaches. It was good to go together, and it blessed us to see so many people receive Christ and experience physical and emotional healing.

One day while working in the kitchen, I met a Filipina woman who was a volunteer at King's Lodge. I learned that she is a retired nurse and a strong believer who comes every Wednesday to help with cooking.

"What are you planning to do over Christmas break?" she asked.

"We were planning to go to Birmingham to my friend's home, but they said they cannot host us. So, we decided to stay here at the base."

Right away she said, "I don't usually carry much money, but this morning I felt led to bring a 100-pound note. Just now, God spoke to me that I was to give you this money to help you with expenses during Christmas break."

I just met this woman and God did a miracle through her! I am always amazed by the means he uses to bless us.

In mid-January, I heard through my sister, Asenla, that my mom had fallen and broken her leg. She was then admitted to a local hospital for an operation to repair her shattered bone.

When I told Tai, my face was streaked with tears. "I don't know what to do. I feel helpless, being so far away. I really wish to go and take care of my mom, but it's impossible for me to go now."

"Does she have the help she needs?"

"Yes, my brother and sisters and my in-laws are taking care of her, and I'm so grateful to them. I can only pray for my mom."

"Then pray for her faithfully. Our prayers are as important as the care she's getting."

Because of my work in the kitchen and hospitality department, I understood the importance of caring for the needs of others. I enjoyed helping serve our weary guests, making their rooms clean and comfortable, and praying for them before they arrived. I just wished I could show such kindness to my mother in her time of need.

I felt like God was using this time to take me to another level in my spiritual life. I could feel his presence daily. He said to me to be thankful in everything, to have a positive spirit in everything, to speak positive words and think positive thoughts. Sometimes when I was tempted to judge others, I thought of how I could bless them and bring glory to God.

One day I met a woman named Bindu, a UK resident who was born in India. She is not a believer, but that didn't hinder our growing friendship. She said she enjoyed spending time with me and talking about her two sons and one daughter.

I told her that despite growing up in a Christian family, I did not have the experience of truly knowing Christ as a young child. I talked about how my life later transformed after I embraced Jesus Christ as my personal saviour. Bindu was listening carefully, and she started talking about her experiences.

"Amongla, my husband encourages me to go to a temple, and I have gone to several. But whenever I go, I don't feel peace or joy. I feel like everybody is looking at me, and the way some men look at me is very bad. I don't feel secure.

"I also went to different churches to see what's happening in the Christian world. People were worshipping with beautiful songs. As they worshipped, they seemed so happy and at peace. I started to go to church as well as to a temple."

As Bindu and I spent more time together, I shared freely about the love of Jesus. She said, "The love I receive from you, I have never received from my temple friends."

I told her this love reflected the love I received from Jesus. She always seemed interested to hear more about Jesus. She asked me to pray for her and her family in Jesus' name. I could only imagine how God was going to move in her life and that of her family.

Chapter 13
Joy and Grief

One morning I received this word from the Lord: "There are angels being assigned to your situation, and new revelation and dreams will begin to increase."

A week later I received another word: "Be open to rearranging your schedule and be flexible as there are some good surprises for you."

The first surprise came because of our daughter's prayers. The unstable weather in England made it difficult to walk to and from school. One rainy day, she said, "Mom, I am tired. I wish we had a push car for you to take me to school."

"Ask Jesus to give us one," I replied.

"Okay, I will pray every day."

And she did. Two weeks later, as my husband was walking Aroma home from school, a man ran towards him and said, "I want to talk to you. I often see your daughter and your wife walking, and I have an extra push car. I would like to give it to your daughter."

Tai was stunned. "Thank you. That's very generous."

"I am glad to give it to her."

Tai wondered, *Who is this person? He is a stranger to us.* When he brought over the push car, we both were astonished. It was an answer to our daughter's prayer. As the scripture says, our heavenly Father knows what we need. He even knows our desires. Mathew 7:7 says, "Ask and it will be given to you; seek and you will find; knock and the door will be opened to you."

In the next few weeks, God began opening all kinds of doors for us to love our neighbours in Nuneaton. We met a young woman who was crying by the roadside. She told us that her family had kicked her out of their home. We bought her a burger and some coffee and shared the love of Jesus. We explained how precious she is to God. She smiled at us, and we asked if we could pray for her. She said, "Yes, please." That day she accepted Jesus, and we had a powerful time of prayer.

After that, we met another man sitting on the road. He told us, "I have no place to stay. I am not from UK. I came here to be with my girlfriend who is from England, but she left me."

We talked with him about the love of Jesus and salvation. We asked if he wanted to receive Jesus. He prayed a confession prayer. We also prayed for a place for him to stay. A few minutes later a man came up to him and offered him housing. We were amazed at how quickly God had answered our prayer.

Another man we met on the roadside said to us, "The last time you guys prayed for me, I was paralysed in half of my body. I was not able to move my left arm. But after you guys prayed, I got healed. Now I am so much better, Thank you!" He, too, accepted Jesus Christ as his personal saviour.

Every Saturday, we went out for evangelism—meeting homeless people, talking to shopkeepers, and greeting our neighbours. Everywhere we went, we shared the love of Jesus and prayed for people. So many people were receiving Jesus, and soon others from King's Lodge joined our evangelism team. I thanked God for prompting me to start this weekly outreach. It always is God's heart to reach the lost.

February 12, 2019

Today as I woke up, I noticed I had missed several calls from my sister Yashila. I rang her back, asking why she had called.

"We are on the way to Dimapur to see Mom. She is seriously sick. Our sister Asenla is with her now."

I immediately made a video call to Asenla, and I could see her face streaming with tears.

"Mom is becoming weaker. She cannot breathe freely."

"Can you put her on the phone," I pleaded.

When I saw her, it broke my heart. She looked so frail and helpless. Oja (mom), don't worry. I will pray for your healing."

Mom responded with a very small voice. "Thank you, Amongla. I am becoming weaker."

I asked my sister to touch Mom, and we all prayed together for miracle healing. When my husband returned from classroom, I shared about my mom, and my husband asked, "What shall we do? Should we return to India?".

I said, "We will not go, but let's trust God for a miracle." The next day again I called my brother, Dr. Lanu. He was holding mom in his arms at the time. He said, "Don't worry. She is just feeling weak. She will be all right." I emailed many prayer partners to ask them to pray for Mom. That evening, I called Asenla and she said, "Mom is feeling better; praise God!" Tai and I continued praying for her that night. In the morning, we got another good report on her health. Three days later, Asenla called to say Mom is doing much better than before. "She is singing revival songs and hymns. She is very happy."

I thought back to a time more than twenty years ago when mom was seriously ill. It was right after I joined Y. I was told that there was no hope medically for my mom, but God added years to her life. It was like what happened to Israel's King Hezekiah when he was dying (2 Kings 20:5–6). God said, "Go back and tell Hezekiah, the leader of my people, 'This is what the Lᴏʀᴅ, the God of your father David, says: I have heard your prayer and seen your tears; I will heal you. On the third day from now you will go up to the temple of the Lᴏʀᴅ. I will add fifteen years to your life. And I will deliver you and this city from the hand of the king of Assyria."

A month after my mom's illness, I received a word from the Lord during my quiet time. It said, "Rise above and trust that God is moving in your life no matter what it looks like." Then I had a dream in which I saw a woman inside a coffin, and that woman asked me for water. I barely slept after that, and I got up hoping that was not my mom's coffin. I shared my dream with Tai, and we prayed together. Then I called Asenla, asking how mom was doing.

"She's doing okay. Would you like to talk to her?"

"Oh yes, I will do a video call."

When Mom popped up on the screen, she looked very happy. She sang a beautiful hymn by heart, something I'd never seen her do before.

"How do you know this wonderful song?"

"The Holy Spirit is helping me." Then she burst into another song about how "Jesus died for me on the cross of Calvary."

I was overcome with tears of joy. I had never seen my mom singing like that. I could see the joy in her face. I told her, "I am so glad that you have salvation. How are you feeling?"

"Amongla, I am so happy, and I have peace in my heart, which I never experienced before. I see the stars, and my world full of light. I am rejoicing in the presence of God. The only thing that would make me happier is having you here. When are you coming home?"

I couldn't give her a clear answer. But from that moment, I began to miss my mom deeply. I told my husband, "Let us ask God to give Mom a long life. I want to see her during Christmas. I want us to be together with my parents at Christmas." And that is what we prayed.

On March 10, I woke up from a dream about all our family coming together in India. My body felt heavy with pain, and I wondered what happened to make me feel so different in my spirit.

I went to the dining hall to get our breakfast, and when I returned, my daughter Aroma said my phone had been ringing. When I looked at it, I saw many missed calls from my family and neighbours. My heart started beating. Something must be wrong.

I dialled my sister Asenla, and when she answered, her voice was weak and shaky. "Oya Among, mom passed away."

My heart seemed to stop at that moment. I didn't know what to say, so I shouted "Oja" (mom) over and over. I said, "I am so sorry that I could not make it to be with you. Go in peace and be with Jesus. One day we will meet in heaven." Those were my last words to my mom. I was so shocked, I felt numb.

I saw my mom's dead body through video inside the beautiful coffin with flowers. I could hear many people singing hymns for her, and it was so hard to be away at a time like that. I wept openly, and my husband and daughter also began crying when they saw me in tears. I felt like I could do nothing to help or honour my mother. Her funeral was in my village of Molungkimong. All I could think was that she was waiting for us to celebrate Christmas together.

Mom had been sick for many years, but dad took good care of her. On the day Mom died, she had some breakfast, then took a bath with the help of my sister, Asenla, and my niece, Purlemla. She told my dad not to leave her alone, so my sister and niece helped her to the bedroom to get dressed. Moments later, she went peacefully to be with the Lord.

During my season of grief, I was often comforted by the words of Psalm 23. "The LORD is my shepherd, I lack nothing…"

As word spread about our loss, friends from King's Lodge came to visit and pray for me. Some took care of our daughter; others sent flowers and cards. My mom was a simple woman of God. She was generous and hospitable, and a great cook. She rarely got enough rest because she was always helping my dad with their five kids. She raised us with the Word of God and encouragement, making sure we were dressed up for Sunday school.

Whenever I think of Mom, Proverbs 31 often comes to mind. I want to dedicate that scripture to her.

"A wife of noble character who can find? She is worth far more than rubies. Her husband has full confidence in her and lacks nothing of value. She brings him good, not harm, all the days of her life…she gets up while it is still dark; She is clothed with strength and dignity; she can laugh at the days to come. She speaks with wisdom, and faithful instruction is on her tongue. She watches over the affairs of her household and does not eat the bread of idleness. Her children arise and call her blessed; her husband also, and he praises her: 'Many women do noble things, but you surpass them all.'"

I praise God because my mom is in a better place with Jesus.

I praise God that my mom finished well.

I praise God for my dad, my siblings, and my in-laws, who helped my mom in her final days.

I praise God for my husband and my daughter, who comforted and encouraged me in many ways.

I praise God for my family, relatives, neighbours, and friends who made my mom's funeral beautiful.

Chapter 14
Homeward Bound

For days after my mother's death, I sat in our room, overwhelmed with grief. I didn't go out, and I felt such pain that I rarely ate. I spent those days talking with my family over the phone. I didn't want any visitors, but my friend Sofia from the Netherlands wouldn't take no for an answer. She stopped in regularly to pray for me and see if she could help in some way.

She was so kind and sweet. One day she said, "Amongla, you need to go out and get some fresh air. Let's go for a walk."

I shook my head. "I don't feel like going out."

"I know you are grieving, but it's not good for you to cut yourself off from the world."

She was right. Though I felt no desire for social interaction, I slowly began to reengage with our community. Our friends had been so comforting. They prayed for us, brought food, and gave much encouragement.

My British friend Helen, whom I worked with in hospitality, also came to spend time with me and

Aroma. She said, "We need you, Amongla. Whenever I am with you, I feel the presence of God. You have made so many contributions here at King's Lodge, starting with your cooking and hospitality work, but especially the evangelism in Nuneaton town. What a legacy you are leaving here."

I needed to hear that. When you're grieving you sometimes feel like your life doesn't really matter. Helen hugged me as she was getting ready to go. To my astonishment, my 4-year-old daughter said to her, "How can you go without praying for us?"

Helen smiled and said, "You're right, Aroma!" She prayed for us on the spot. I was so pleased that my daughter knew the importance of prayer.

The next day, my Indian nonbeliever friend, Dipti, came to visit me. I messaged her that my mom passed away, and when she learned that I had closeted myself in our room for several days, she said. "Amongla, you need to go out to get some fresh air. I want to take you and your daughter to McDonald's."

"That's nice of you to offer, but I don't want to go out."

"I want to go out!" said Aroma. "I would love to go to McDonald's."

When I saw my daughter's eagerness, I knew I couldn't say no.

"Okay, Amongla," said Dipti, "You and Aroma need to get ready."

We had a delightful time together at the McDonald's in Nuneaton town. Dipti and I ate and talked, while Aroma bounced around the restaurant's play area. This outing lifted my spirits, and it deepened my friendship with Dipti.

She started to invite me and my daughter to her home, and she welcomed me to pray for her family. She often said she felt very comfortable around me. I thanked God for using me to reach people with his love and encouragement.

Seven days after my mom's passing, I finally joined in community worship and my work duty, as well. An elderly woman, who works in member care at the campus, was very kind and encouraged me not to rush back to work. Sometimes I ran to my room and cried. I worried about how my dad was doing. When I called him, he said he had been sick, but was feeling better now. How I wished I could be there to wrap my arms around him.

A few weeks later, as our time in England was nearing its end, I felt a desire to visit Leicester, the city that launched William Carey into missions in India. This great man, who was described as "a candle in the dark," had been pastor of Harvey Lane Baptist Church in Leicester. God called him to serve in Calcutta, and he started ministries that changed the face of India.

We had no transportation to get to Leicester, so I prayed, "Lord, if it is your will, please open the door for our family to visit." His answer came a few days later. We had met a couple from Leicester named Pathak and Priscilla, and to our surprise, they invited us to spend a night at their home. Once again, God had made a way for us.

When we reached their home, we were shocked. It was a massive, beautiful house. After a short rest, our friends took us sightseeing, including visits to William Carey's historic sites. In the evening, we prayed together. Priscilla declared, "Jesus, we believe you are visiting us and that you brought this family to be with us." I felt so encouraged by her prayer.

The next day, we celebrated Easter Sunday at their church. Then Pathak and Priscilla took us to lunch at an Indian restaurant. It had been a long time since we had eaten such good Indian food. When they drove us back to Nuneaton, I thought of two expressions that described this wonderful weekend. God answers prayer, and God is good all the time.

We were now just weeks away from our return to India, and I was getting excited. Though I enjoyed our season in England, especially the one-on-one times with my daughter, I missed friends and family back home. Though I was focused on our departure, I had an unexpected and blessed time with Aroma a few weeks before we left.

The King's Kids leader at our base invited my daughter and I to do children's ministry at upcoming meetings of the Christian Medical Fellowship. "We really need your help, so please pray about it," he pleaded. He had asked me before, and I hadn't responded. This time Tai and I talked and prayed about it, and I finally said okay.

The three-day national conference was held at a lovely hotel. When we arrived, my daughter said, "Mom, I am super excited about helping you. I hope there will be a lot of kids coming here with their parents."

She helped me set up play areas and plan activities. During the conference, our team divided the children into age groups, and we taught them Bible stories, songs, and prayers. It was great fun, and we felt privileged to be able to serve so many kids. Those three days were truly a God-ordained time.

It made me particularly grateful because sometimes I get so busy at the YWAM campus that I don't get to spend quality time with my daughter. Those few weeks, I enjoyed seeing her grow and mature. Though she is just five years old, she sings her songs, dances beautifully, and loves to pray. I am so grateful for our daughter.

June 1, 2019

On this day, a not-so-funny thing happened to me. One of my friends gave us a country chicken to eat for lunch. I popped it into the electric cooker in the kitchen, then went back to our room to do some work. Much later, I remembered that the chicken was cooking, and I ran to the kitchen. It was full of smoke. The burning chicken caused the fire alarms to start ringing. All over the campus, people hurried towards the exits. Once the chicken was removed, the fire danger was over, but I felt very nervous and embarrassed. I could not even go to the dining hall for my dinner. I asked Tai to bring food for me. I thought he would be upset with me, but he said it was okay. "You just need to be careful next time."

The next day I went to the campus leadership team and asked forgiveness for what I had done. They said, "Amongla, this has happened to many people, not just you. So, you don't have to feel sorry." One thing I learned during those few months at King's Lodge, is that the community doesn't judge people for mistakes made. That is one of the beautiful things about our YWAM culture.

Our last big adventure in England was to go with other School of Biblical Studies students to visit the British Museum and Library in London. I was stunned by the massive size of the museum and the incredible treasures within it. The library contains some of the oldest Bibles and religious writings found anywhere in the world.

On June 27, we woke up about 5 a.m. and said farewell to King's Lodge. Some of our friends came with us to the Birmingham Airport to bid us goodbye. Aroma was crying. She had made some good friends here, and we knew she would miss them.

The flight to Mumbai was on time, and we praised God for the many ways we experienced his grace here in England. What a privilege to serve our living God!

On the flight, we talked about our best memories from this journey.

"I enjoyed the school and the people here, but I will not miss the cold weather," Tai said with a wink.

"I have gotten used to it," I said. "India will feel hot by comparison."

"I will miss my friends," said Aroma with tears still streaking her face.

I was scheduled to teach in a DTS shortly after our return to the Lonavala base. All the way home, I prayed and processed about the possibility of handing over my role as campus DTS coordinator. It had now been more than 25 years since I joined DTS as a student.

We can put our hope in a role or a ministry to be the answer to fulfilling our dreams and living life to the fullest. Ministries have seasons. You either get bored with a role that you've been in too long, or you change too often and tend to live in the stress of development. We as a family continue seeking God for the right decision. What he wants us to do is not always what we might think we want to do.

Chapter 15
Father Heart

We settled back into our base Lonavala campus, but as good as it was to be home, I still didn't feel peace in my spirit. I knew it was time for me to hand over my responsibility as DTS director.

Even though I felt certain it was the right move, I still wrestled with the decision. When I thought about staying on, a word popped into my mind that I knew was from God. It said, "If there is no transition, the DTS will die." Then came an even stronger word: "God is going to wake you up to new understanding; you will wonder why you didn't know this before." This was the confirmation I needed.

I communicated with our campus leaders and then handed over my leadership of the department to younger staff, those who I had been coaching over the last few years. I planned to continue mentoring staff for the DTS department and serving the campus in whatever ways I could. The campus leaders accepted my decision and were very positive in the way it was officially communicated. I felt ready for the next steps, but I had no idea how hard they would be.

Just a month after we returned from England, my sister Asenla called to say that our dad was sick. After Mom passed, he became weak physically and finally decided to travel to Dimapur for treatment. He thought the problem was an ulcer, but when my sister Asen and my brother, Dr. Lanu, took him to the hospital, he was diagnosed with gastric cancer. This news sent shockwaves through our family, and we all rallied to support him.

When I called my father, he said, "Amongla, I have faith in God. He will heal me."

"Yes, he is a great healer, but you are not a young man. You need help."

The problem was I couldn't come to help just then. I was still teaching in the DTS, and our family was getting ready to move into another rented house. As I processed what to do, I grew increasingly restless and could barely sleep at night.

The next time I called my dad, I pressed him about his health. "Be honest with me Oba (father), how are you doing?"

"Don't worry, Amongla. I am feeling better. I believe God will heal me."

He didn't sound better, but I had to trust God with the situation.

"Let's pray right now," he said.

We both prayed over the phone and afterward, dad told me he was very happy. That evening my niece, Naro, called me to say that our family was going to do a conference call so that we could see each other and have time to worship and pray together for Obo (grandfather). It was a powerful time of prayer as a family. Although we were in different places, we all felt the presence of God.

I contacted friends to ask them to pray for Dad too. Having such a network of prayer support finally gave me the peace I needed. It was hard enough to lose my mom. I didn't think I could handle the loss of my dad.

Monsoon season in India and the heavy rain, especially in Lonavala, was dampening my spirits even more than usual. Pounding rain seemed to be coming down nonstop. In August, our washing machine broke down—so I had no choice but to wash our clothes by hand and try to dry them inside. It took at least a week to dry most clothing items. My misery continued as the washer repairman kept putting us off. After nearly two months, I poured out my impatience and anger at him over the phone. When the repairman did finally come to our home, God spoke to me that he wanted me to treat him with kindness. So, I offered him tea and snacks and listened as he told me his troubles. The result was that he didn't just repair our washer; he replaced it with a newer and better model. God's ways are always best!

In August we also completed the contract on our new rental house and began our monsoon move. Our landlord was a devout woman of another faith woman who worked in a local bank. Though the rent was expensive for us (Rs. 16,000 a month), it was the best we could find near our ministry location. We got her to agree not to sell the house or raise the rent for the next two years.

The new house has two bedrooms and a small kitchen and living room. Our friends helped us move our furniture and household items in the heavy rain. My sister, Atenla, came from Pune to help us, and we cooked a nice rice and curry meal to thank all who helped us. Soon the new house was ringing with laughter, and that brought us joy and some new friendships.

Most weekends, we'd invite people over to our house for a meal and fellowship. I love to cook for our guests and my husband makes sure we always bless them with encouragement and prayer. When we married, we agreed that we wanted our house to be open for hospitality, whether we had food enough or not. We would always share whatever we had.

God's Refreshing Word

On September 1, my siblings and I did another conference call to pray for our dad. Although we live in different places, we feel a sweet sense of unity whenever we pray, seeking God for my dad's health. On this day, our families fasted and prayed, and I was delighted that our Aroma, now 5, joined us. When someone asked if anyone had a message from the Lord, Aroma said: "Yes, I do! God gave me Psalm 2 as an encouraging word for grandfather."

I was shocked. How could a child that young be familiar with the Psalms? God can use even the children. I later called up my dad and gave him that scripture reference. He felt so encouraged and astonished that a little girl delivered the Word to him.

A few days later, a local pastor asked us to seek God concerning his family. He said, "My wife is very sick, and I believe we are going through some kind of spiritual battle. It's been a difficult time for us. Could your family please come to Pune and pray for us? We need you."

Tai and I promised to pray for them, but we weren't sure we could go to Pune.

"What do you think we should do, Tai?"

My husband gave it some deep thought. "Remember that tomorrow our campus will have a general clean-up day. We don't want to skip out on our responsibilities, but when people need urgent prayer, we need to make that a priority. Ask God what we should do tomorrow."

God spoke clearly to us, telling us to go to Pune to Pastor's house. It takes more than two hours by car to go from Lonavala to Pune. So, we asked permission from our work duty supervisor, and we headed off to Pastor's house. He and his wife were eagerly waiting for us the next day.

The pastor started sharing first. "We've been under a lot of stress. We've had some discouraging situations in the church, and we've also had a lot of sickness." We listened for a few hours as they poured out details of what they had been going through. We finally stopped them so that we could pray and ask God to give them a word of encouragement.

On the way back, we discussed what had happened and concluded that we had made the right choice. "We can make up the work duty, but I believe we made the right move in going to see them then." Tai nodded. "We couldn't have done that kind of ministry on the phone."

The Decision About Dad

Our family had booked tickets to Nagaland for the end of November, hoping to have a long visit with dad over Christmas and New Year. But it soon appeared that I would need to move up my travel plans. Dad was still receiving treatment in Eden Hospital in Dimapur but without much improvement. On October 3, we got another call saying that dad was becoming much weaker.

I still had a week of teaching to do in DTS, and it was hard for me to cancel or reschedule. I called my brother for his advice, and he encouraged me to wait. But afterwards, my Aunty called to say, "Amongla, it will be good for you to come home now."

I still had one day of teaching for a class of 40 students. I felt so conflicted, I asked the Lord to give me peace. Somehow, I got through that day, and early the next morning, my brother called. This time there was urgency in his voice. "Oya, (elder sister) you must come and see dad right away. His life is coming to an end."

I began to weep. With a choking voice, I replied, "Okay, I will call Atenla. Hopefully, she can come too, and we can book the flights together."

Tai and Aroma came with me to Pune and said goodbye at the airport there. We almost didn't make it, as suddenly as there was heavy rain, which snarled traffic into the city for hours. Cars on both sides of the highway were not moving. Then it occurred to me, that we need to pray! I prayed loudly, and my daughter joined in at equal volume. She started saying, "Halleluiah Jesus help us." After about twenty minutes, we were able to cross a flooded street and get to the airport. God had indeed protected us!

Atenla and I arrived at Dimapur airport at about noon, and family members rushed us to Eden Hospital, where our dad was being treated. When we entered Room 212, we were surprised that so many people were sitting around with him. One of them was my brother, Dr. Lanu, and his face looked gloomy.

I immediately took my dad's hand and called, "Oba" (dad). He did not answer, but he tried to open his eyes to see us, and a tear rolled from his eye. He looked so weak and frail. I told Dad we wanted to pray for him. I sensed he knew that Atenla and I had reached him, because I could see his tears coming from his eyes.

For the next ten days, I was with him in the hospital. I often held him in my arms, weeping and praying for him. The muscular man I knew as a youth was now thin and pale. His deep brown eyes were dim from age and illness. I hoped and expected every day that he would get better. Whenever the doctor came around, I asked if there was any sign of improvement. I asked over and over again, hoping he could give some ray of hope on my dad's condition. Instead, dad lapsed into unconsciousness. I prayed that my Oba would speak out, for I was longing to hear his voice.

Dad was not getting better. The doctors tried their best to help by changing his medicine, but we saw no improvement. He was becoming weaker by the day and his hospital bill was mounting. Then, by some miracle, dad responded *aowa* (yes) when I called his name. It was just a tiny ray of hope, but I felt like it was an answer to prayer just for me. I was so thankful for the relatives and neighbours who supported us so generously with their time, prayers, and resources during this painful season.

My brother, Dr. Lanu, and his wife, Dr. Achi, decided to discharge my dad from the hospital since he wasn't making any improvement. They said we could take care of him at their home. He seemed to be in a coma, and we had to give him liquid food through his nose. I cried out to God not to take him. It had been only seven months ago that my mom passed away. None of us could bear the thought of losing our father too. Many people were coming and praying with us.

One of those who came in to pray was my brother's neighbour. I was sitting with my dad that morning when she came to pray. She said, "I have a message for your family. Last night I had a dream, and in the dream, your dad said he wants to speak farewell. But he cannot go to be with Jesus because your family will not release him. So please release him. Your family should release your dad."

I nodded, but my heart wasn't ready to let him go. All that day, I told the Lord, "I don't want to release him. Couldn't you please give him a few more years?"

Later that day, my daughter Aroma sent me a WhatsApp message, a photo of a beautiful card she made. Under the big letters MOM, it said, I love you so much. I am missing you so much." It gave me a warm feeling of hope, which I needed since I was getting so little sleep. Over the last two weeks, our family had not once left dad alone. I was with him in the evening, and he vomited for a few minutes. I could not look at him. It broke my heart to see him struggle like this.

About midnight my sister-in-law, Dr. Achi, came and told Atenla and myself, "Go take rest; I will take care of tonight along with your cousin."

I went to another room intending to rest for just a few minutes, but I slept from 1 to 3 a.m. I was awakened by Atenla, who shouted, "Oya (elder sister), dad is becoming more serious. Get up quickly." I jolted out of bed and ran to dad's bedside. I held him and noticed his face looked different. His breathing was fast, then it slowed to a faint whisps. All of us were there now, and as his breathing slowed, I started shouting "Oba" (dad) again and again. I held onto his chest, hoping I could somehow keep him alive. But at 4:45 a.m., my much-loved father finished his life. It was a Saturday morning, October 19, 2019.

Chapter 16
Through the Storm

I wasn't prepared for the outpouring of love and respect that touched our family because of dad's passing. We arranged to have his body taken to our home village, where my mom was buried. Soon, dozens of neighbours, relatives, church members and friends came to the house to pay their respects. My dad was laid out in a beautiful casket that was full of flowers. He wore a new suit that was covered by our Ao Naga tribe's traditional shawl. All through that first night, people came and went, singing songs and sharing memories.

With the help of our relatives, friends and neighbours, we put on a feast for all who came to the funeral. There were great mounds of rice, meat, and vegetables for all the visitors to enjoy. As I wandered around my childhood home, I still couldn't believe my parents were gone. They died within seven months of one another, and that awful season was like an earthquake in my life.

Dad served as a deacon in our church for 21 years, so he was known and loved by many in our village. His body was kept on display in our living room. I wished this was all a dream. My dad was no more! I still could not accept it.

On Sunday morning, before the church service, the pastor arranged a funeral service for my dad. Many church members expressed gratefulness for his many good deeds and kindnesses. The next day, he was honoured by relatives, friends, church elders, and village council members. One elder spoke about dad's commitment and faithfulness in his work. "He was an example to many people. He left a good legacy as a hard worker, and as a man who walked in integrity. He was also fun, loving, and responsible." It was encouraging to hear the affirmations from many people, but it made me miss my father even more.

Dad had an orange grove, which he loved and nurtured. As his health failed, he hired people to maintain the orange trees. In his last month of life, he expressed a desire to cut back the grass around the trees. So my brother, Dr. Lanu said, "Let's honour his memory by hiring some people to do the work."

When dad's friends and neighbours heard about our brother's plan, they said, "Let us help." Altogether, 48 people came to help cut the grass. They worked hard, and I wished dad could have been there to see all that was done to care for his special place.

Some of my best memories of dad were when we went fishing together. He loved fishing, and it was in that setting that we saw his fun-loving and nurturing side. He saw fishing as a way of teaching discipline to his children and other young friends. He had lots of friends of different ages. He treated them all with equal respect, and that's one thing I admired about him.

His life was anchored in Jesus, and he encouraged us to walk in the fear of the Lord. He challenged us to be truthful always and to live with integrity both at home and in our work. He often led our family in prayer, and he encouraged us to love and help one another.

Dad was not happy with me when I joined Y. He thought that living by faith instead of having a salaried job was not going to work for me. He was just concerned as a father. But when he saw how well the Lord provided for me, he came and asked forgiveness. He said, "Amongla, I was foolish in trying to discourage you from joining Y. I am sorry, and I have asked God to forgive me." Every time I think of his words, my eyes fill with tears for I know my dad was touched by God's faithfulness to our family.

After the funeral, though I was still grieving, I wanted to be available to serve the Lord there. One day I was praying for our family, and God led me to pray for other parents. Soon I was approached by one of my cousins who said, "Amongla, I need your help. My son is struggling and is drinking too much alcohol. Could you please counsel and help him to change his life?"

Although it was difficult for me to help others when I was hurting so much myself, I knew God always wanted me to be prepared when ministry opportunities came along. When I prayed, immediately felt God wanted me to help this young man, believing that one day he would have a great testimony. He said to me, "I want to change my life." I told him that only God could do that. I later connected him with a ministry called "Halfway Home," which was started by two of my friends. They willingly accepted him into their program.

I stayed in Dimapur for three months. During that grieving season, God gave me several opportunities to minister to young people there. It blessed me to share the Word of God with them and to lead them in prayer for salvation and changed lives.

In late November, Tai and Aroma arrived from Lonavala to spend the Christmas holidays with my family. My heart filled with joy at the sight of my 5-year-old daughter pulling along her own luggage. As we returned to the family home, she was full of questions about Nagaland and our extended family. This would be our first Christmas without my parents, and I choked up at the thought of it.

Thankfully, my brother and sisters got to spend lots of time together over the Christmas holiday, and we shared lots of special memories. Ecclesiastes 3 says, "There is time and a season for everything." I had my season of grieving, but I emerged from it so thankful to have had such good parents.

On January 30, 2020, I officially handed over my role as DTS director. My passion was always to train and equip young leaders and release them for the mission.

The night after I made this transition, I had a disturbing dream. Tai noticed how shaken I was and asked me to describe it to him. "What God is trying to speak?" he said.

"In the dream, I saw the Y Lonavala campus. The building's pillars were collapsing; people were screaming and trying to run away. I saw many friends looking scared and running around. One of our elders, Mac, was trying to fix the building, but it was completely damaged. Then I saw a group of people come toward our campus, and I asked, 'Are you here to help us rebuild?' At that moment, I heard a voice from above say, 'Amongla, it will stay like this for some time.' That was my dream."

"I think it is a very significant dream, and we need to pray about it," said Tai. We immediately prayed together, but I still felt no peace or had no sense of the dream's interpretation. I later shared it at our leadership meeting, and we prayed too. But I still felt restless, wondering what this dream meant.

At the time, I was largely unaware of the coronavirus pandemic that was spreading around the globe. I heard that it had started in China. That seemed so far away that I did not take it seriously. But within a few weeks, the virus reached our part of India with terrible effects. In all, 45 million Indians were afflicted by the Covid 19 virus and over 500,000 died.

In this painful season, I kept processing, praying, and seeking God for what he wanted me to do for his kingdom. The word I received was, "Hold on and get ready as new doors of opportunity are going to open quickly. You will encourage others as God confirms things he has been speaking to you. Be patient and confident to step out and take risks as God is perfecting new things in you, and he is with you. Things are now lining up for new assignments and realignment for this new season."

This word was so encouraging, especially in light of all the gloom and doom in the world that resulted from the pandemic. I didn't know exactly how the Lord would lead us, but I felt new confidence it would be in his perfect time. He is always faithful to respond to us.

In March of 2020, the Lonavala campus was in a full-blown crisis. At the time, we had 90 students and about 60 staff. The government was scrambling to impose restrictions to slow the spread of the disease. People everywhere were afflicted by worry and stress about the virus as well as the economic and social impact of the impending lockdowns.

Our campus leadership team met and decided to encourage all the staff and students to go back home. We were running a Discipleship Training School and a School of Biblical Studies. In that troubled time, many students likely wondered if would ever see one another again.

The reason we encouraged them to go home is that we did not know how long it would take for the lockdowns to be lifted. Besides that, it was increasingly difficult to buy food. Only about 30 people decided to stay at the campus and weather the storm.

God reminded me of my dream and the sight of people fleeing as the building was collapsing. During the first week of the government lockdown, we were anxious because we did not have many groceries on hand. We tried to manage what we had, and a few shops were open for a limited time each day. It felt so eerie to see the usually busy streets virtually empty.

Many of our neighbours were fearful about going out to shop because they had to queue up with others who might be carriers of the virus. Most of the time, we stayed inside, too. We didn't visit with anyone during the first two weeks of the lockdown. We had little to eat, and the food that was available at local markets was getting very expensive. It hurt to see our little daughter going hungry, but most people in our area were facing the same struggles.

As we watched the news and prayed, we knew God was going to open doors of opportunity. He led us to begin praying Psalm 91 because it's such a powerful promise of help in troubled times. Then we started reaching out.

As hard as things were for us, they were much worse for homeless people living in local slums. During the lockdown, God gave us opportunities to help feed them and to show the love of Jesus. Many in India don't have regular salaries. They survive on whatever income they can earn each day. We tried to help as many of these financially stressed people as we could.

The most surprising opportunity God gave us was with the local police. My husband I had asked the Lord what he wanted us to do. One day, while visiting my friend Jen, we talked about our burden for reaching local people, and God led us to reach out to the Lonavala police.

They were seen as enforcers of lockdown restrictions, so their level of stress was even greater than usual. We asked friends to contribute money to make 100 appreciation cards. I made the cards with my own hands. We also gathered small gifts that friends contributed like hand sanitizers, masks, and sweets. We asked permission from the local police chief, and he seemed grateful for our support.

On August 15, which is India's Independence Day, a few of us arrived early in the morning to honour the police as they hoisted our national flag. At that event, we distributed our small gifts among the police. The officers were so pleased that they invited us to come into their offices. It gave us a wonderful opportunity to tell them how much we appreciated their service to the people. We were grateful for the way this door of relationship opened.

God did many wonderful things during the lockdown season. The journey was hard, but we experienced God's faithfulness in his protection and his grace. Our campus was able to distribute grocery provisions to thousands of families, thanks to generous donations that poured in. Doors opened for our staff to reach out to tribal groups in our community that we didn't know existed among us. Even when we couldn't go out to meet people in person, he used us in different ways. My husband and I lost count of all the people we counselled and ministered to over the phone.

God has since inspired me to write about the experiences of my journey with him. The hardest times became some of the best of times. I grew in faith so much during the pandemic, as I saw God move in seemingly impossible circumstances. I praise God for his unconditional love. I praise Him for how he has provided and guided us. As Ephesians 3:20–21 says, "Now to him who is able to do immeasurably more than all we ask or imagine, according to his power that is at work within us, to him be glory in the church and in Christ Jesus throughout all generations, for ever and ever! Amen."

I am grateful to know and serve a God who hears us and answers our prayers. The motto in Y is "To know God and to make him known." It has been a remarkable journey of faith. As I look back, I see how God has met myself and my family in a great variety of circumstances. He has been with me both in joy and in grief. He has comforted, opened doors, healed, and met financial needs in ways that I could not have imagined. He has taken me from humble village surroundings as a young child and been with me through a wide array of life experiences around the globe. I have seen his faithfulness again and again. God is good, no matter what, and we can trust him with everything.

About the Author

Amongla Setefano is from Nagaland, in the northeast part of India. She is married to Tai Setefano, from the island nation of American Samoa. Amongla and her husband are the parents of one daughter, Aroma. Before joining fulltime missions, Amongla completed her B.Th. (Bachelor of Theology) degree at Working People's Bible College in Dimapur, Nagaland. She also holds a certificate as professional life coach. Amongla is currently studying for her M.Div. (Master of Divinity) degree through external studies at Faith Theological College in Dimapur, Nagaland.

Amongla has been serving with Y for the last 26 years. Her current role is as a member of the Leadership Team of the UofN (University of the Nations) in Lonavala, India. Her heart is to see the next generation discipled, equipped, and released to service for Christ. Amongla mentors DTS (Discipleship Training School) leaders, does counselling and coaching for members of her organization, and teaches in various DTS programs. She also enjoys cooking with different varieties of food, hospitality, serving people, and doing one on one meetings with those who need a listening ear, encouragement, and prayer.